Your Private Oil Well ?

FOREWORD

This book is a must for anyone wanting to run their vehicle on biodiesel or who just wants to know what the stuff is.

It will take you through an education process which, at the end, could leave you deciding to make your own. Either just for your own vehicle or as a business venture.

Full do-it-yourself instructions are given, for home production or for something more extensive. For those wishing to take their first steps towards challenging the OPEC oil producers, a review of purpose-built mini-process plant is provided.

You don't need a Chemical Engineering degree to understand this book! Information is presented with great enthusiasm and in an easy-reading style. Furthermore, extensive references to relevant websites allow the more curious reader to follow up his or her own research interests.

The book deals with both the environmental and economic issues, and outlines the potential to move towards a more sustainable transport future. The tax implications of biodiesel production are also discussed.

Most importantly throughout the book, for those of a practical persuasion, the health and safety "do's-and-don'ts" of biodiesel home production are emphasized.

Although the book was written in the UK by a Brit, it is oriented more towards the biodiesel scene in the USA. But, apart from some of the data that relate particularly to the USA, the vast bulk of the book is just as relevant to Europe and elsewhere.

For those interested in the biodiesel scene this is a reference book that will be informative and entertaining to read, and could pay for itself many times over.

Dr. Geoffrey Whittle – Engineer U.K.

Legal Statement

DISCLAIMER AND TERMS OF USE AGREEMENT

The author and publisher of this "The Book on Biodiesel" and the accompanying materials have used their best efforts in preparing this Merv's biodiesel handbook. The author and publisher make no representation or warranties with respect to the accuracy, applicability, fitness, or completeness of the contents of this 'The Book on Biodiesel'. The information contained in this 'The Book on Biodiesel' is strictly for education purposes. Therefore, if you wish to apply ideas contained in this 'The Book on Biodiesel', you are taking full responsibility for your actions.

Every effort has been made to accurately represent this product and its potential. Even though this industry is one of the few where one can write their own cheque (in terms of earnings, there is no guarantee that you will earn any money using the techniques and ideas in these materials. Examples in these materials are not to be interpreted as a promise or guarantee of earnings. Earning potential is entirely dependent on the person using our product, ideas and techniques. We do not purport this as a "Get Rich Scheme".

Any claims made of actual earnings or examples of actual results can be verified upon request.

Your level of success in attaining the results claimed in our materials depends on the time you devote to the program, ideas and techniques mentioned your finances, knowledge and various skills.

Since these factors differ according to individuals, we cannot guarantee your success or income level. Nor are we responsible for any of your actions.

Materials in our product and our website may contain information that includes or is based upon forward-looking statements within the meaning of the securities litigation reform act of 1955. Forward-looking statements give our expectations or forecasts of future events. You can identify these statements by the fact that they do not relate strictly to historical or current facts. They use words such as "anticipate", "estimate", "expect", "project", "intend", "plan", "believe" and other words and terms of similar meaning in connection with a description of potential earnings or financial performance.

Any and all forward-looking statements here or on any of our sales material are intended to express our opinion of earnings potential. Many factors will be important in determining your actual results and no guarantees are made that you will achieve results similar to ours or anyone else's, in fact no guarantees are made that you will achieve any results from our ideas and techniques in our materials.

The author and publisher disclaim any warranties (express or implied), merchantability, or fitness for any particular purpose. The author and publisher shall in no event be held liable to any party for any direct, indirect, punitive, special, incidental or other consequential damages arising directly or indirectly from any use of this material, which is provided "as is," and without warranties.

As always, the advice of a competent legal, tax, accounting or other professional should be sought.

The author and publisher do not warrant the performance, effectiveness or applicability of any sites listed or linked to in this 'The Book on Biodiesel'.

All links are for information purposes only and are not warranted for content, accuracy or any other implied or explicit purpose.

Index

CHAPTER 4: Glycerine 123

Introduction

Hello, I'm Merv Rees.

I am about to take you on a journey through the intriguing world of biodiesel with its many twists and turns –

Sometimes I relate the state of play of fuel resources or the lack of them, cover many surprising areas overcoming problems, plus we will have fun and avoid the dangers we find on our way, experience sheer excitement of producing your very own fuel in the form of biodiesel, whether you need it to run your vehicle or a fleet of them, or to generate electricity, or perhaps heat for your home or factory.

Whatever the use, the independence gained from within these pages will, I'm sure, please and inspire you with the many opportunities that will unfold for you.

So let's go -

Fossil fuels

Fossil fuels, which include petroleum-based fuel, the primary fuel source used for powering the diesel engine are depleting. Due to this decline, alternatives need to be made in order to not only meet the demands of global society, but to also improve upon the health of people, nature and the environment.

For this reason, more and more organizations around the world are adopting a green thumb by switching to biodiesel, a renewable fuel that is primarily comprised of vegetable oil or animal fats, and works in compression-ignition engines.

Biodiesel is not a new invention. In fact it has been around for over a century, but it never gained the same popularity as petroleum fuel until the demand for biodiesel increased, particularly in the past 1-2 decades, when the world's demand for liquid energy grew substantially.

Furthermore, biodiesel has also become a more favourable alternative as it promotes a number of benefits such as:

- Continuous surplus of agriculture commodities, such as the demand for soybeans in the U.S. (Soybean oil is primarily used to create biodiesel in America).

- Regional subsidy programs.

- Tax credits to biodiesel consumers.

- Unlike petroleum fuel, biodiesel is CO_2 neutral, which means that throughout its entire cycle, biodiesel neither increases nor decreases the level of carbon dioxide in the air.

- Biodiesel emissions do not contain sulphur or aromatics, which makes its emissions lower than petroleum diesel, preserving better air quality.

- It is safe to mix biodiesel with petroleum diesel at any level. This means more and more consumers are opting for biodiesel blends, such as B20, which costs no more than petrodiesel.

Of course, along with the benefits of biodiesel, there are a number of disadvantages. One such disadvantage is the lack of biodiesel outlets, although the number of biodiesel distributors and retailers are growing in the U.S. and overseas. When compared to the total consumption of petroleum diesel, biodiesel barely makes a mark in the industry as yet, but the situation improves daily.

Part of the problem with biodiesel is that not many people are aware of its existence, or know very little about it to make the change. That is why it's important for you to understand everything there is to know about biodiesel, so you can discover the alternative that's out there waiting for you right now.

This book, **'The Book on Biodiesel'**, has been designed to do just that – give you the key to open your mind to the "green" thinking alternatives of biodiesel.

Within its pages you will discover what's new in the biodiesel world of today and the future, and provide you with all the essential information there is to know about biodiesel including:

- Answers to the questions you have about biodiesel.

- Where you can purchase biodiesel.

- How to make your own biodiesel fuel.

- How you can benefit from using biodiesel.

- How you can get involved in the biodiesel industry.

and much more, including any negative aspects, and how to fix them.

Knowing everything about biodiesel is the only way you will ever fully understand the unique benefits it can provide to the economy, the environment and to human society.

This knowledge is the first step you will make on the road to finding out how you can take action to make the world a cleaner, healthier place. Let nothing throw you, be pleasantly surprised, keep an open mind and enjoy the miracles surrounding us all daily.

Kat-Kat
Drying off after a swim in the Pacific Ocean!
Purrrr – Flc!

Chapter 1
What is Biodiesel?

Biodiesel is an alternative combustible fuel or fuel additive for diesel engines. It is non-toxic, biodegradable, and virtually free of aromatics and sulphur.

This is because its primary components are domestic renewable resources such as vegetable oil and animal fats. Thus, Biodiesel is the mono-alkyl esters of fatty acids that result from animal fats or vegetable oils.

In other words, biodiesel is the end result of the chemical reaction caused by mixing vegetable oil or animal fat with Methoxide.

The latter is made up from an alcohol, usually methanol and a catalyst such as Lye [Caustic Soda – NaOH – (Sodium Hydroxide) or KOH (Potassium Hydroxide)] is also necessary to separate the various layers of methanol, glycerine, and sometimes soap and/or water, in order to create the finished product biodiesel fuel.

No petroleum exists in biodiesel, but biodiesel can be mixed with petrodiesel at any level.

This allows it to be compatible with most diesel engines, without requiring these engines to need any modifications.

Furthermore, due to the fact that biodiesel is renewable fuel, and can replace petroleum based diesel in present engines, it's no wonder that biodiesel is considered to be one of the future possible replacements for fossil fuels, which is currently the world's chief source of transportation energy.

In addition, since biodiesel can be sold and transported by using the present infrastructure, the production of this biodegradable fuel is rapidly increasing, particularly in Europe, Asia and North America. However, even though biodiesel production is increasing in certain parts of the world, it still only represents a small percentage of actual fuel sold. Nevertheless, the number of large transport fleets that use biodiesel in their fuel is rising, and every year more fuel stations are working on making biodiesel accessible to consumers.

Common Biodiesel Questions and Answers

Since you may not be familiar with biodiesel, the following are answers to some basic questions you may be wondering about which will help further your understanding on biodiesel before going into detail about the subject.

For example has Biodiesel been approved in the United States?

Biodiesel has been approved in different parts of the world including the United States.

Biodiesel is legally registered as both an independent fuel and fuel additive with the Environmental Protection Agency (EPA).

It also meets the clean diesel standards set by the California Resources Board (CARB). Biodiesel is recognized as a suitable alternative fuel by the U.S. Department of Transportation (DOT) and the Department of Energy (DOE).

Moreover, the amount of biodiesel that is sold in the U.S. is rising substantially every year. To give you a better idea of the sales increase, the following are the U.S. annual biodiesel sales volume estimates from 1999-2004 as determined by the National Biodiesel Board (NBB): and you can take similar snapshots throughout the years to see its rapid growth since then.

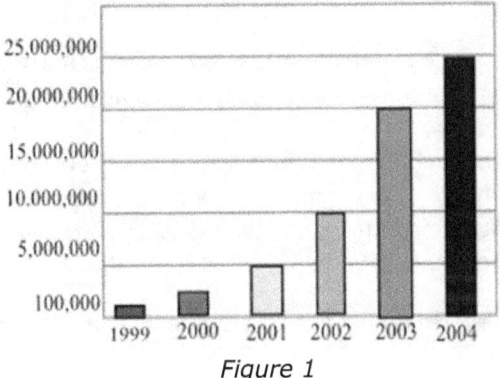

Estimated Early Years Annual Biodiesel Volume in Gallons

Figure 1

Biodiesel can be used as a pure fuel, and it can also be added to petroleum diesel at any ratio.

For instance, while some transportation operating fleets run purely on biodiesel, others run their vehicles on B20.

B20 is not straight biodiesel, and is a term that specifies that the fuel used is 20% by volume biodiesel and 80% by volume petrodiesel fuel. Therefore, if the fuel were B40 it would be 40% by volume biodiesel and 60% by volume of petrodiesel, and so on.

Pure biodiesel is more environmentally friendly. Currently it could be more costly to buy unless you produce it yourself; you would require to add additives in colder climes specifically designed to support B100 in order for it to run at its best, at all times.

However, by blending the two diesel fuels, i.e. biodiesel and regular diesel, there are still many noteworthy environmental bonuses. Consumers can still benefit the environment without paying too much, as most engines require no modifications, and can run perfectly with B20 or any other mixed ratio.

More information on this subject can be found in Chapter 6.

Is using biodiesel the same as running an engine on raw vegetable oil?

Due to the fact that biodiesel is made from renewable resources, and that those resources make up a large percentage of the formula, you may be wondering if using biodiesel is the same as using untreated straight vegetable oil in your vehicle. The answer – plain and simple – is no.

In order for biodiesel to run a diesel engine, the oil must have gone through transesterification, a 'refinery' process that involves mixing the oil with an alcohol (methanol) along with a catalyst we call 'Lye' (sodium hydroxide) = (caustic soda) to create a reaction that allows the removal of glycerine, the main by-product of biodiesel. Furthermore, to ensure proper performance, fuel-grade biodiesel must follow industry specifications known as the ASTMD6751 in the US or EN14214:2005 in Europe.

However – Just to be awkward

Straight Vegetable Oil running – Yes it is possible.

It is possible to use untreated S.V.O without converting the straight vegetable oil into biodiesel. A lot of people with mainly commercial vehicles are doing so already and yes quite a lot of private vehicles also.

However you need a conversion kit, an extra fuel tank, a three-way valve, sometimes two of them for some systems, to switch the fuel back and forth from regular diesel to untreated S.V.O; and with a heat exchanger system in place, as it is best to preheat the vegetable oil to reduce viscosity.

It appears that the fuel injectors themselves help towards this end, from the friction effect of the actual injection of oils into the engine combustion chamber.

Talking of injector pumps, at the time of writing, Bosch injector pumps seem to give fewer problems with untreated SVO, but you're still asking for trouble, because of the 'polymers, fats and acids' that build up in your systems and can cost a fortune in time and replacement of fuel injector pumps.

Pre-heating your oil is sometimes managed by diverting the engine's cooling system through water pipes within the prepared fuel tank, and/or heating cables around oil filters and fuel line heat exchangers, so improving the viscosity of the oil which helps prevent waxing, that you do not get with biodiesel, because the glycerine and soaps etc are removed.

Sometimes a percentage of petrol is mixed into the vegetable oil to help against waxing and filter plugging; a very dangerous practice.

In adverse conditions ever more volatile mixtures are added for increased cold weather usage.

OK so that's roughly how the system is set up, but actually running the system is quite easy once you are rigged out. What usually happens is this, the main fuel tank is given over to vegetable oil and a new smaller tank is fitted to carry regular diesel.

Let us say in the morning your vehicle is ready and you are switched over to the regular diesel from the last time you used the vehicle, recheck the position of the three-way switch before starting your engine.

Right, start up in normal fashion and drive off, after a few miles when your engine is good and hot and hopefully your vegetable oil has had chance to warm through after standing out all night, you simply switch your 'three-way' switch over to your main vegetable oil tank and journey forth. When you know you're going to stop you switch back over to your regular diesel so your fuel lines are preloaded with diesel for when you wish to travel on again.

So there you have it, mostly used by commercials! Plus in UK you need to contact Customs and Excise and get yourself a **form EX103**.

. . . . **But remember it ain't Biodiesel which is vastly different with its many advantages!** So please read on ...

But Hey – To each their own!

Currently, biodiesel is the only alternative fuel that has passed the 1990 Clean Air Act Amendments, having fully completed the health effects testing requirements.

Therefore, biodiesel fuel that is up to ASTMD6751 standards, and is registered with the Environmental Protection Agency (EPA), is legally recognized as a fuel for diesel engines and can be sold and distributed. Raw vegetable oil, on the other hand, does not meet the specification for biodiesel fuel, so it cannot be registered with the EPA, making it illegal as a fuel.

Are there different types of Biodiesel?

In essence, there are three different types of biodiesel:

1. Biodiesel created from straight vegetable oils (S.V.O) with methyl-esters (Methanol)

2. Biodiesel created from waste vegetable oils (W.V.O) with methyl-esters (Methanol)

3. Biodiesel made with ethyl-esters (Ethanol)

The first two types of biodiesel generate the same end-result, as each must go through the transesterification refinery process and meet the specification of the U.S. ASTMD6751 in order to be considered pure biodiesel fuel.

The third type, on the other hand, is a tricky process that also goes through transesterification, but is still being experimented on.

More about the different process of making these three forms of biodiesel will be discussed in Chapter 3.

What are the basic ingredients of Biodiesel?

In order to create biodiesel, regardless of the process, there are three main ingredients:

1. Renewable Feedstock:

a. Straight vegetable oils (corn oil, cottonseed oil, canola oil, mustard oil, soybean oil, a variety of edible rapeseed oil, palm oil, etc.)

b. Waste oils (restaurant frying oils, etc.)

c. Grease (grease from restaurant grease traps, float grease from wastewater treatment plants, etc.)

d. Animal fats (pork lard, beef tallow lard, etc.)

2. Alcohol:

a. Methanol or b. Ethanol

3. Lye:

a. Sodium hydroxide... (NaOH) caustic soda

b. Potassium hydroxide (KOH)

Biodiesel that is produced in the United States is primarily made from soybean oil and methanol, as these are the most popular feed stocks in the US, and soybeans are one of the country's chief crops. Biodiesel made from soybeans is sometimes called by other names such as soy methyl esters (SME), methyl soyate and soydiesel. In addition, experiments are being done in Idaho to test the effectiveness of blending rapeseed esters with ethanol. The effect produces what is known as rapeseed ethyl esters (REE).

In Europe, however, the majority of biodiesel produced is made from rapeseed oil (a chief crop) and methanol. This mixture is known as rapeseed methyl esters (RME).

What does Biodiesel look like?

Biodiesel has a similar viscosity (thickness) to petroleum diesel, and in its pure form it looks from

a nearly clear to an amber-yellow range of colour liquid.

I'm holding up a jug so you can see what biodiesel looks like. The biodiesel is a lighter colour and the darker layer at the base is glycerine and other waste traces.

Are engine modifications required for biodiesel?

Engine modifications are not required for any diesel engine vehicle, or any other diesel-burning equipment such as oil heat boilers, that uses the biodiesel blend B20.

However, although blends that are higher than B20, as well as pure biodiesel can be used in many engines that were constructed after the year 1994, slight modifications such as engine timing are usually necessary to all diesel engines to ensure top performance with minimum NO_x emissions.

However, having said that, diesel engines of any age can use pure biodiesel or a mixture of any ratios blends, providing you take care to change any perishable parts of the fuel system for modern materials.

Rubber is the problem pre 1994, as in the fuel tank filler and pipe line connections. However wherever you find a rubber or perishable material, just change them for a synthetic product like plastic and all will be fine.

Filters need to be checked and cleaned regularly, especially at first because biodiesel will dissolve all the deposits lining your fuel system left behind from using fossil fuels (regular petro diesel). I generally advise if you have not got a fuel line filter which you can easily get at to clean, you simply have one fitted quite cheaply with see through construction.

After a short while of using biodiesel, either 100% pure or a mix in any proportions of biodiesel and regular diesel, the problem fades away as your fuel system goes clean. As does your engine and its emissions thus proving you are doing your bit for your own and your family's environment.

Why can't Biodiesel be used in cars powered by unleaded or lead fuel?

First of all, vehicles that are powered by unleaded or lead fuel require gasoline because they have spark-ignition engines, and do not function in the same way as the compression-ignition engines found in diesel vehicles. As the name implies, spark-ignition engines (ICE) require spark plugs to ignite the fuel that powers the engine. Thus, the fuel used for this type of vehicle needs to be extremely thin and explosive to work effectively, i.e. petrol.

On the other hand diesel engines, or compression engines as they should be known, do not use spark plugs, but super-compressed air, which ignite the fuel. The compressed-ignition engine is normally sturdier and heavier, as it is designed to run on viscous fuels such as petro-diesel (fossil fuels) or bio-diesel fuel, which is generally derived from vegetable oil.

Can Biodiesel be used for any other purpose aside from running engines in diesel vehicles?

Yes. Although powering diesel engines is its primary use, biodiesel has been tested and is being used already for heating oil.

Heating Oil

Washed biodiesel can be burnt in most standard oil burning heating stoves, though some may require some adaptation, or by blending with regular fuel oil as biodiesel is less viscous than conventional fossil based heating oil. This is both cheaper and better for the environment.

What is not considered Biodiesel fuel?

Any biodiesel blend such as B20 is not a pure biodiesel fuel as it is mixed petroleum diesel, e.g. B20 is 20% biodiesel and 80% regular diesel.

Raw oils are not biodiesel fuel because they have not gone through the transesterification process.

Diesel blends derived from ethanol, known as E-diesel, are not considered biodiesel blends, even though they are environmentally friendly and show future promise.

Where can I purchase a Biodiesel car?

There are a number of dealerships across America, or any other parts of the world for that matter which sell new and used diesel engine cars that are fully compatible with biodiesel fuel. To gain a better insight into your options, check out the section on "Biodiesel-Compatible Car Models," located in Chapter 10.

Where can I purchase Biodiesel fuel?

Biodiesel fuel is distributed and sold by retailers across the United States, Canada, United Kingdom, Europe, Australia, Asia and in many other parts of the world. Aside from the following information, more details on where you can purchase biodiesel is discussed in "Quantities and Availabilities" in Chapter 6.

Distribution

For the many farmers and transportation fleets that use biodiesel, there are more than 1,400 petroleum distributors in America that have biodiesel and biodiesel blends. Some of these distributors include large organizations such as Growmark™ and Cenex™.

The vast majority of biodiesel distributors will usually deliver biodiesel to their consumers in whatever form the customer wishes. For instance, in pure biodiesel fuel or a biodiesel blend like B20.

You can get a better clue as to where biodiesel distributors can best be found in the United States the United Kingdom and most countries around the world through the internet, indicating the distribution locations, because as soon as I update my maps they get out of date, mind you this is an improving situation daily which should be good.

Retailers

If you don't need a distributor, and are looking for a retailer that sells biodiesel at a pump near you, there are hundreds of retail stations, including both gas stations and fuel docks that currently make blends of biodiesel available to the public.

Obviously it depends on which country you are in, but again check the web to find the areas, and where you need to pick up your supplies

The number of biodiesel retailers and distributors continues to increase across the U.S., and you will find updates, as well as a list of companies that supply biodiesel in the U.S., along with their contact information, by visiting the NBB – Member Fuel Producers/Marketers site at:
www.biodiesel.org/buyingbiodiesel/producers_mar keters/default.shtm

More to the point, another way you can obtain biodiesel is to buy the ingredients and equipment and creates your own fuel.

Creating biodiesel fuel is a simple yet detailed process, and to find out more about how you can make your own biodiesel, as well as all of the ingredients and equipment you will need for the procedure, Chapter 3 has all the information you need to get started.

Who uses Biodiesel fuel?

Anyone who has a compression-ignition engine (diesel engine) can use biodiesel fuel to run his or her vehicle. To be a little more specific, here are just a few examples of those who use biodiesel fuel around the world:

- Farmers

- Bus companies

- Food and beverage industries

- Restaurants

- Retail stores

- Construction companies

- Real estate

- Universities

- School districts

- Recreation and tourism

- Military

- Mining

- Parks and recreation

- Haulage companies

- Marine industry

- General public, this list is but a small sample and goes on ever growing.

Just about anyone who uses a diesel engine for any purpose can use biodiesel.

Basically there are numerous companies and individuals that use biodiesel in one way or another, regardless whether or not they are directly involved in production or sale of the bio fuel.

For instance, while a food industry may not make biodiesel, they may supply their waste oil to a company that will use it to produce biodiesel, such as the case of Kettle Foods™, a company based in Salem, Oregon that sells different types of snack foods including organic chips, which can be purchased at a variety of supermarket across the U.S.

Although they don't produce their own biodiesel, Kettle Foods™ has an alliance with SeQuential Biofuels™, which uses the company's waste oils to produce its biodiesel, which they sell at a public pump. In addition, Kettle Foods™ runs its company vehicles on biodiesel fuel.

Farmers

As far as U.S. farmers are concerned, they can benefit greatly from using soy-based biodiesel. For example, some of the benefits include:

- It creates demand to grow their crops for their own personal farm use.

- Soy biodiesel is high quality fuel that provides their equipment with:

  Outstanding lubricity

  Lower maintenance costs

  Longer Life

- The higher the demand for soybeans, the more farmers will gain to improve the prices of soybean.

Schools and Universities

A number of school bus fleets in the U.S. have been switching to biodiesel blends. Some of these school districts include:

- Arlington, County, Virginia School District (B20 since 2004)

- Clark County, Nevada School District (2003)

- Olympia, Illinois School District (B20 since 2002)

- Medford, New Jersey School District (B20 since 1997)

Likewise, universities that are jumping onto the biodiesel bandwagon to improve the health of the environment, its staff and students include:

- Harvard University (B20 since 2004)

- University of Michigan (B20 since 2002)

- Northwest Missouri State University (B20 since 2001)

- University of Idaho (involved in biodiesel research and experiments since 1979)

When all is said and done, currently there are over 400 U.S. fleets using biodiesel commercially. This includes all 4 branches  of the military plus several school districts, numerous city bus systems and even Yellowstone National Park. Main reason, biodiesel is a proven environmentally friendly fuel.

It is also important to note that the vast majority of organizations that use biodiesel do not use pure biodiesel (B100) not because they could not, but as yet supply and demand could not keep up with the vast amounts they require – but I guess the time will come.

The most common form of biodiesel used in the transportation industry is the biodiesel blend B20. This is mainly because it is cost effective, plus engines do not require modifications, and they are seen to be helping with reduction of CO_2 and particulate emissions thereby helping us, and our environment.

You will discover more resources about the benefits associated with using biodiesel in Chapter 6.

A Brief History of Biodiesel

The invention of biodiesel can be credited to three men: scientists E. Duffy, and J. Patrick, who were the first to conduct the transesterification of a vegetable oil in 1853, and the inventor of the diesel engine (1893), Dr. Rudolf Diesel.

However, it was Dr. Diesel who was the true visionary of producing an engine that ran on renewable resources.

Figure 2
Rudolf Diesel

Diesel's first model of his diesel engine, an iron cylinder with a flywheel at the bottom, successfully ran on its own power for the first time on August 10, 1893 in Augsburg, Germany. Seven years later, in 1900, he went on to demonstrate his compression-ignition engine powered by 100% peanut oil at the World Exhibition in Paris, winning first prize for his invention.

Originally, Diesel invented his engine to run on a variety of fuels, some of which included heavy mineral oil, suspended coal dust in water and vegetable oil. However, his hopes to power the diesel engine with these products failed and he didn't achieve success until he featured his peanut oil running engine in the World Exhibition.

After his untimely death in 1913, Diesel's engine continued to run on vegetable oils, until it was modified in the 1920's to run on petroleum-based fuel. Thus, although the diesel engine became popular and accepted around the globe, biodiesel didn't gain the same popularity, and it wasn't long before petroleum diesel became the primary fuel choice for the diesel engine.

Petroleum had with it many financial benefits that biodiesel did not. For instance, it was more available, had government subsidies and was a better price.

Due to these reasons, biodiesel was all but forgotten until the mid 1970s, when fuel shortages began to occur, and interests in developing an alternative fuel to petroleum 2based diesel resurfaced.

Although biodiesel was once again developed, it was still no match for the petroleum industry that continued to be subsidized, making the development of biodiesel as an alternative fuel in the 70's short lived. Even now with the growing concerns of poor air and water quality, as well as global climate change, the biodiesel industry continues its political and economic struggle.

Nonetheless, because many are worried about human health and the environment, the inspiration to develop biodiesel as an alternative fuel for diesel engines is stronger than ever before. More and more people are recognizing the benefits of using a bio-fuel that is created from various feed stocks and recycled vegetable oil. These components make biodiesel a participant in the active carbon cycle, as its feedstock production contributes to the reduction of greenhouse gas build-up, which also helps reduce the effects of global warming.

Today, in the United States, the numbers of fleet operators that are making the switch to biodiesel are rising, and include a handful of fleet operators such as transit buses, airport shuttles, heavy-duty trucks, marine and national park vehicles and boats, and many more.

Yet even so, the amount of biodiesel consumed in the U.S. accounts for less than 1% when compared to total diesel fuel consumption. This only goes to show that there is still plenty of work to be done in the biodiesel industry if it is ever to become more than just a hopeful alternative to diesel fuel in the future.

Thus, the history of biodiesel began with Dr. Rudolf diesel, and even though Dr. Diesel never achieved his goal in its entirety during his lifetime, his invention of the diesel engine and ideas on agriculture has provided our society with the foundation needed to operate on clean, locally grown and renewable fuel.

In remembrance of his vision and first display of his invention,

August 10th

has become

International

Biodiesel

Day

Honouring Dr. Rudolf Diesel

'The Founder of Biodiesel'

Chapter 2

Safety

Safety in relation to the chemicals you will be using and the responsibilities for your own safety and the safety of others. This chapter is for your guidance only you must recheck everything for yourselves.

To make Biodiesel you have to work with DANGEROUS POISONOUS Chemicals. Common sense MUST be used at all times.

You are responsible for your own actions and the safety of yourself and everyone and everything around you!

Safety Drill Advice

Keep telephone numbers of an emergency hospital / doctor, local emergency poison response centre in a prominent location by your phone and wear correct safety clothing, chemically safe gloves, goggles and masks.

Cautions: NEVER mix the Methanol and NaOH (Lye) in a regular plastic bottle as NaOH attacks some types of plastic – If plastic is used it must be to safety standards of 'HDPE 2' (high-density polyethylene).

Once Methoxide (methyl ester) is thoroughly mixed, it is ready to add it to a vegetable oil, to make your biodiesel sample. For that you could use a safe recyclable heavy plastic bottle. Look on the bottle base for this recycle mark:

HDPE

Check out a few bottles around your house; you'll be surprised at the results.

NEVER store unused methoxide (methyl ester). It's not only dangerous, it like plastics, will degrade and your biodiesel will fail to separate from the glycerine etc in manufacture.

Methanol boils at approximately 65°C/148°F. DO NOT mix when the oil temperature is above 54°C/130°F (see figure 11, page 62).

NEVER allow WATER, no matter how little into any steps of this vital and potentially dangerous procedure.

SAFETY – YOU ARE RESPONSIBLE FOR YOUR ACTIONS, AND YOUR OWN SAFETY, AND THE

SAFETY OF EVERYONE AND EVERYTHING AROUND YOU!

Again, these chemicals are dangerous and great care is necessary, even more so if children and pets are around, so you must keep them locked out.

About Methanol

Methanol, otherwise known as methyl alcohol, wood naphtha, wood alcohol, wood spirits, and methyl hydrate, MeOH, CH3OH or CH40 etc. is a flammable liquid and vapour chemical that is extremely poisonous!

IMPORTANT – Methanol is POISON

and cannot be made non-poisonous.

Methanol is Flammable in liquid form or as a vapour.

HARMFUL if inhaled.

Methanol can be absorbed through healthy unbroken skin, killing the nerves.

Methanol - Can affect Whole Nervous System and the Liver.

Methanol - In worse cases cause BLINDNESS, and even DEATH.

It also causes eye and skin irritation, digestive tract upset (including nausea, vomiting and diarrhoea).

You can visit at webpage J.T.Baker.com a top flight company which produces a Material Safety Data Sheet (MSDS) regarding Methanol. *(Source: http://www.jtbaker.com/msds/englishhtml/m2015. htm)*

For more information about proper safety measures when dealing with Methanol, turn to the section on "Safety Clothing Equipment" see page 77.

NB. Non Toxic Ethanol could be used to make biodiesel instead of Methanol.

NaOH Sodium Hydroxide

Purchasing Sodium Hydroxide

- Hardware stores the vast majority of hardware stores will sell Red Devil™ lye, (caustic soda) which is used as a drain cleaner. Just make sure the ingredients are pure sodium hydroxide. (Other cleaners may say they contain lye, but if it's not pure, it won't work when making biodiesel)

- Specialist suppliers of larger quantities. If you do buy in large stocks, make sure it is in a lot of small well sealed plastic containers.

- For larger working quantities (in small units) find on-line.

MORE ON (LYE) SODIUM HYDROXIDE & POTASSIUM HYDROXIDE (KOH)

Otherwise known as caustic soda/lye (NaOH), sodium hydroxide is the preferred choice over potassium hydroxide, because it is easier to obtain and it is often cheaper. However potassium hydroxide (KOH) is easier to use, and the process isn't any different than sodium hydroxide, except that you are required to use 1.4 times as much the amount called for sodium hydroxide. If you would prefer to use potassium hydroxide you can get it from chemical suppliers.

IMPORTANT – sodium hydroxide and potassium hydroxide are dangerous chemical that are corrosive!

They react with acids, water and other materials including

aluminium, zinc and tin.

IF INHALED: <u>seek Urgent & Immediate Medical Advice.</u>

Both sodium hydroxide and potassium hydroxide can cause severe burns if in contact with skin wash well with soap and water for 15 minutes.

Should it get into eyes, wash with copious amounts of running water, taking care to wash under the eye-lids, wash for 15 minutes and seek Urgent and Immediate Medical Advice.

If either chemical is swallowed it could be FATAL!

Ingestion (Swallowed)

NEVER INDUCE VOMITING! Give large quantities of milk if available or water. If a person is unconscious, never give anything by mouth. Get immediate medical attention!

Source: *J.T.Baker.com* now also re-sited at *www.mallbaker.com*

Material Safety Data Sheet (MSDS) regarding sodium hydroxide.
www.jtbaker.com/msds/englishhtml/s4034.htm

Material Safety Data Sheet (MSDS) regarding potassium hydroxide.
www.jtbaker.com/msds/englishhtml/p5884.htm

IT'S A FUNNY OLD WORLD

There is no doubt that chemicals are dangerous, and here we want to help our environment and ourselves by making our own bio-friendly fuel.

To do this we gather together our ingredients and are proud to be able to use up used cooking oils, which a lot of the time is tipped down drains, causing no end of problems, or thrown into ditches etc. Restaurants have to pay to get it taken away, so a reliable free collection service is very welcome.

The 'Biodieselers' come along and take the problem away for free, yes to help themselves, and as long as its legal why not? Everyone wins!

Well now the oil is secured, let's say we have all equipment at whatever level, we need, but now we have to obtain what some call **the 'nasty bits'**.

Yes – 'The Chemicals'!

DANGEROUS MATERIALS used in the production of biodiesel where information in Material Safety Data Sheets is required knowledge. Read them and the warning labels affixed to the sides of the containers or found in the chemical analysis attached to product.

- Methanol Alcohol

- Isopropyl Alcohol

- Phenolphthalein Indicator

- Phenol Red Indicator

- NaOH (caustic soda)

- KOH- (Red Devil™ Lye)

Each and every one of these chemicals must receive your respect and understanding, so you can safely enjoy your new hobby or business.

Each chemical has to have its own MSDS (Material Safety Data Sheet) for you to read and then the knowledge will keep you safe if you show it the respect it deserves.

Therefore, some direct info:

LINKS FOR MATERIAL SAFETY DATA SHEETS WEBSITE

Source: J.T.Baker.com and / or
www.mallbaker.com

Methanol
www.jtbaker.com/msds/englishhtml/m2015.htm

Isopropyl Alcohol
www.jtbaker.com/msds/englishhtml/i8840.htm

Phenolphthalein
www.jtbaker.com/msds/englishhtml/p2015.htm

Phenol red
www.jtbaker.com/msds/englishhtml/p2059.htm

NaOH (Caustic Soda)
www.jtbaker.com/msds/englishhtml/s4034.htm

KOH- (Red Devil Lye)
www.jtbaker.com/msds/englishhtml/p5884.htm

ORGANIZATION

Cleanliness – Keep your work place tidy, put empties into bins, rags into outside bins (inflammable especially if been wiping up spillages, of oil or methanol)

Sand – Have an open sand box for use against fire or mopping up slippery spillages.

Fire Extinguisher – Advice should be obtained from your local fire station, on Safety Procedure and Equipment.

Make sure fire extinguishers are correct ones for oil or alcohol situations, and the situations in your own work station.

Make sure the whole family knows the fire drill which your local Fire Authorities will gladly advise you all for FREE!

If unfortunate enough to have a fire, sound the alarm and make sure everyone evacuates the building.

Ventilation – Methanol is an alcohol, as is isopropyl, and their fumes are potentially a danger, hence good ventilation, and keep tops on containers and in a cool place. Mixing methoxide can be extremely hazardous so make sure you wear safety gear whilst keeping well ventilated.

Back Injury – Avoid back injury or sprains, when lifting heavy objects.

- Learn the correct lifting posture.

- Keep a neutral spine that means keeping your spine straight.

- Stand close to object you are about to lift with your back straight.

- Now bend your knees keeping back straight.

- Use leg muscles to lift by steady firm pressure.

- Never jerk on object, and if too heavy get some help and still follow same procedure.

- Protect Hands.

- Be safe you're worth it. (I am a qualified 'Sports Fitness & Training Therapist' as well as an engineer).

Chapter 3

How to make Biodiesel?

OVERVIEW

There are three basic approaches that can be taken to produce biodiesel and they are as follows:

Base catalyzed transesterification of the oil with alcohol. Conversion of the oil to fatty acids and then to biodiesel with acid catalysis.

Direct acid catalyzed esterification of the oil through methanol.

Most of the biodiesel that is currently produced is done through the first process – base catalyzed reaction – as it is considered to be the most economic. This process results in the catalyst (sodium hydroxide or potassium hydroxide) splitting the oil into two parts:

Course Glycerine (by-product of biodiesel)

Biodiesel (fuel that can be used to power a diesel engine)

The way it works is the catalyst is dissolved in alcohol (Lye and Methanol), and then added to the oil or fat. The oil and catalyst are mixed and are constantly and thoroughly blended for two hours into preheated vegetable oil, temperature (see figure 11) no higher than 130°F or 54°C, which speeds up the reaction time. With the increase of both temperature and pressure the transesterification reaction becomes catalyzed. The average overall reaction time varies depending on the method of production, but generally 8 hours is given.

Usually excess methanol is used to speed up the process, as well as ensuring that the fat or oil completely converts to esters. But a word of warning, too much methanol can react in reverse in some situations.

Once the process is complete the glycerol needs to be split from the biodiesel, and all excess alcohol must be removed through either evaporation or distillation, and of course biodiesel needs to be filtered and washed.

The following three diagrams display the process in which the base catalyzed transesterification takes place. They show three ways to give you the best understanding of the basic biodiesel manufacturing process.

This diagrammatic chart shows the avenues in various manufacturing situations in the making of biodiesel.

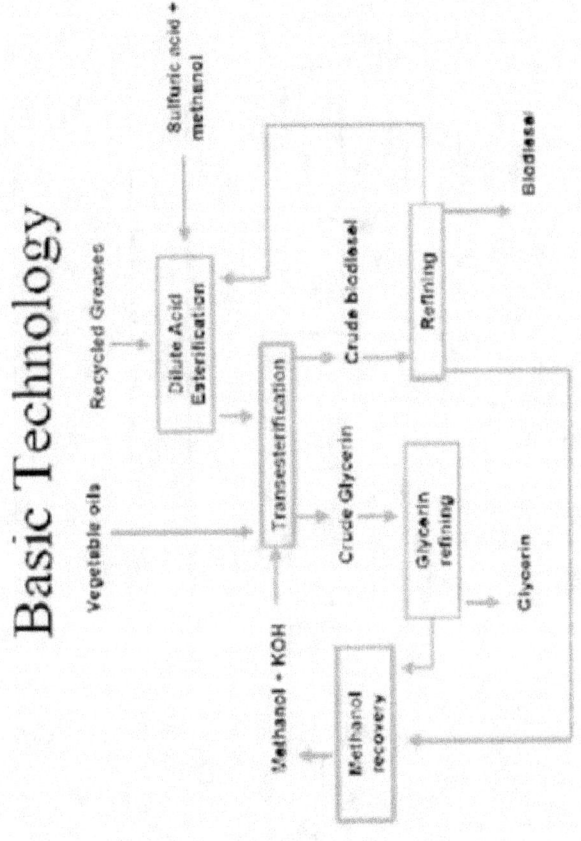

Figure 3

Process Chart

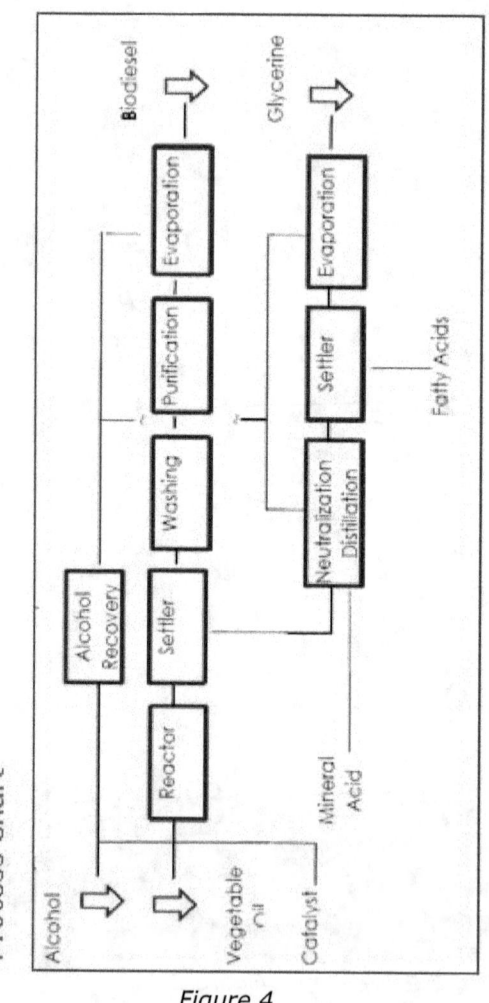

Figure 4

Here I've drawn a diagram which shows that the amount of biodiesel created in one batch depends on the total amount of ingredients used.

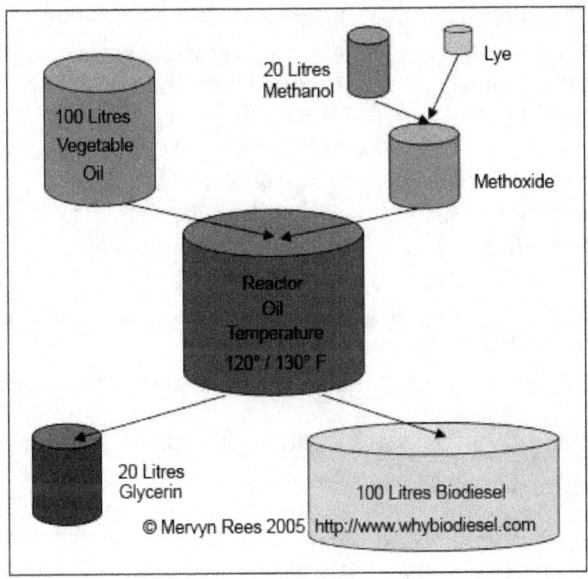

Figure 5
Merv's Diagrammatic Illustration

Therefore, as my diagram reveals, if you wanted to produce 100 litres of biodiesel the following would be the result:

100 litres of oil + 20 litres of methanol = 100 litres of biodiesel and 20 litres of raw uncleaned glycerine.

How does the transesterification process work?

The process known as transesterification works by substituting alcohol (methanol) for glycerine during the chemical reaction caused through the use of lye (sodium hydroxide) as a catalyst.

Simply put, animal fats and vegetable oils are triglycerides, and within triglycerides there is glycerine. During the biodiesel process when the oil is mixed with the methoxide (blend of alcohol and lye), the oil turns into esters and separates from the glycerine, which eventually sinks to the bottom, leaving the biodiesel to float on top.

The entire transesterification process happens in 3 stages.

1. A single fatty acid chain bonds with methanol, after breaking off the triglyceride molecule, and creates a methyl esterase molecule.

   This leaves a diglyceride molecule (DG), made up of two chains of fatty acids that are bound through glycerine.

2. One of the fatty acid chains breaks off the DG and bonds with the methanol to create another methyl ester molecule, which results in a monoglyceride molecule (MG).

3. The monoglycerides that have been created are converted to methyl esters to complete the process.

What is 'FFA'?

Free fatty acids or FFA are acids that form from heat, oxidation or water from the foods that have been cooked in the oil.

FFA is the additional components in the waste oil that have separated from the oil's triglycerides, and have left behind monoglycerides, diglycerides and free glycerine.

The amount of FFA in waste oil depends on how long it was heated for; the longer it stays hot, the more FFA's are produced.

What is Titration?

To determine the FFA content in the W.V.O, and the amount of lye that will be required to neutralize it, titration is the process that must be performed. Titration determines the pH, which is the acid-alkaline level in the oil. As a rule of thumb, if the level reads a value of pH7 it means it's neutral. Values lower than pH7 indicate increasing acidity, and levels higher than pH7 are alkaline.

In order to test the pH level of W.V.O (waste vegetable oil) you can use an electronic pH meter, pH test strips or phenolphthalein, all of which can be purchased from biodiesel equipment suppliers, or garden centres, swimming pool and Spa suppliers.

However the real trick is to determine the precise amount of lye needed per litre of WVO to give the required result, for unlike SVO which is constant, WVO alters according to the type and amount of use it has had.

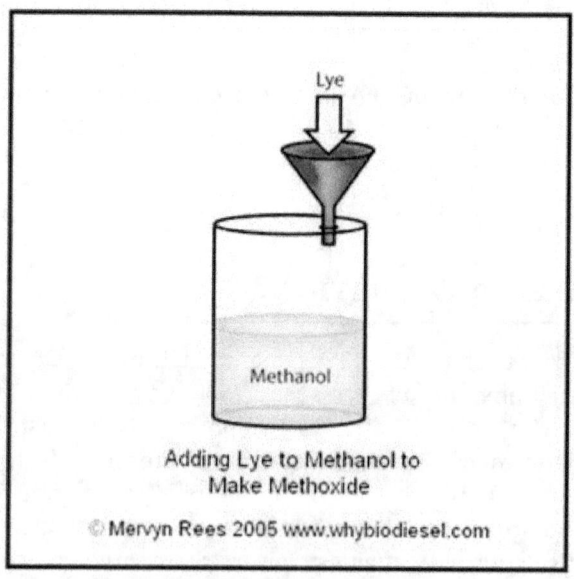

Diagrammatic Illustration

You will soon discover how to handle all of this within these pages, as I take you through it step by step.

MATERIALS

Methanol (IDA – Industrial Denatured Alcohol)

Purchasing methanol depends on many factors according to your location. Here in the U.K. where I live you first register with
http://customs.hmrc.gov.uk/

- Larger working quantities find online.

- From Specialist suppliers of industrial chemicals.

About Methanol
- This information written elsewhere previously – It's Important!

Methanol, otherwise known as methyl alcohol, wood naphtha, wood alcohol, wood spirits, and methyl hydrate, MeOH, CH3OH or CH4O etc. is a flammable liquid and vapour chemical that is extremely poisonous!

IMPORTANT –

You can visit at webpage J.T.Baker.com/ mallbaker.com a top flight company who provide a Material Safety Data Sheet (MSDS) regarding Methanol.

(Source:http://www.jtbaker.com/msds/englishhtml/m20 15.htm)

For information about proper safety measures when dealing with Methanol, turn to the section on "Safety Clothing Equipment".

NB. Ethanol normally non toxic is a straight chain alcohol and has many usages and could be used to make biodiesel instead of methanol.

NaOH Sodium Hydroxide

Purchasing Sodium Hydroxide

Hardware stores (the vast majority of hardware stores will sell Red Devil™ lye, (caustic soda) which is used as a drain cleaner. Just makes sure the ingredients are pure sodium hydroxide. (Other cleaners may say they contain lye, but if it's not pure, it won't work when making biodiesel).

Specialist suppliers - for larger quantities. If you do buy in large stocks, make sure it is in a lot of small well sealed plastic containers;

otherwise opened containers soon oxidize and become less effective.

For larger working quantities (in small units) find online.

More on (Lye) Sodium Hydroxide & Potassium Hydroxide (KOH)

Otherwise known as caustic soda/lye (NaOH), sodium hydroxide is the preferred choice over potassium hydroxide, because it is easier to obtain and it is often cheaper. However potassium hydroxide (KOH) is easier to use, and the process isn't any different than sodium hydroxide, except that you are required to use 1.4 times as much the amount called for sodium hydroxide. If you would prefer to use potassium hydroxide you can get it from chemical suppliers.

IMPORTANT – Sodium Hydroxide and Potassium Hydroxide are dangerous chemical that is highly corrosive!

They react with acids, water and other materials including aluminium, zinc and tin.

If inhaled, get urgent medical advice.

Both can cause severe burns. If in contact with skin, wash well with soap and water for 15 minutes.

Should it get into your eyes, wash with copious amounts of running water, taking care to wash under the eye-lids, wash for 15 minutes and seek urgent medical advice.

If either chemical is swallowed it could be FATAL!

Ingestion (Swallowed)

Never INDUCE VOMITING! Give large quantities of milk, if available, or water. If a person is unconscious never give anything by mouth. Get immediate medical attention!

Source: *J.T.Baker.com* now www.*mallbaker.com*

Material Safety Data Sheet (MSDS) regarding Sodium Hydroxide.
www.jtbaker.com/msds/englishhtml/s4034.htm

Material Safety Data Sheet (MSDS) regarding Potassium Hydroxide.
www.jtbaker.com/msds/englishhtml/p5884.htm

Still more about Lye

Lye (sodium hydroxide or potassium hydroxide) is one of the most essential ingredients in the production of biodiesel, because it is the catalyst used in the transesterification of the oil.

Lye works by absorbing the atmosphere's water, which means it is hygroscopic. That being the case, when you purchase lye, make sure it is fresh and it is tightly sealed in the container at all times. It must be kept dry in order to work properly.

Furthermore, lye also takes carbon dioxide from the atmosphere, which carbonates it.

Therefore, when you open the lye to weigh out the measurements you need, try to do it as quickly and safely as possible, and close the container and add the lye to the methanol immediately.

The problem with lye becoming carbonated is it becomes weaker. So although you can still use it for making biodiesel, you will need to add more of it (approximately 25%). You will know if your lye has become carbonated because it will be white. Non-carbonated lye is almost clear.

When adding lye, it is imperative that you use the correct amount.

If you use too little, some of the oil will remain unreacted when the process is complete, and if you use too much, you'll end up with too much soap, resulting in biodiesel which is difficult to wash.

Quantities of Lye

See Titration for how much 'lye' to use,

i.e. for new vegetable oil or used vegetable oil, and whether you are using NaOH (caustic soda) or

KOH (potassium potash) as a source of lye?

NEW VEGETABLE OIL

You can purchase new, unused vegetable oil from:

1. local grocery store

2. local convenient store

3. baking supply store

4. Supermarket etc.

You don't need a specific brand of vegetable oil; any brand will do, so if you want to purchase the cheapest no-name brand on the market –

Then– **Have a Ball – Knock your socks off!**

EQUIPMENT

The equipment you will require for a small quantity of biodiesel for this homemade recipe includes:

- Heating unit like a 'Baby Burco™' immersion heater/boiler.

- Steel bucket or other suitable container (not galvanized and not tin or aluminium as it will be eaten through) with portable thermostatically controlled immersion heater unit.

- Scales & measuring containers

- HDPE containers

- Temperature gauge 'an old vehicle gauge' will do it.

- Thermometer used as in ... (see figure 11, page 62)

- "Stirring mechanism" old blender etc.

- Siphon pump.

- Beakers for titration (Glass jars)

- Syringes, pipette (eye dropper) (calibrated in millilitres)

- Litmus sticks or papers.

- Coveralls, chemical proof gloves & goggles, suitable respirator.

- Stove or other household equipment

Using your own kitchen equipment if suitable and safe, for small test batches is OK, but do not use your stove and best work out-side. You can purchase a separate sealed flameproof heater from a biodiesel supplier or yard sale. Small test batches can be reasonably controlled with care, using the bain-marie principle of controlling heat and a thermometer.

Use a well-ventilated WORK AREA.

Choosing to use your own stove could be dangerous and not advised, make sure you secure any work area, and have necessary safety equipment immediately to hand, and all mixing of methanol or methoxide is carried out in the open air.

Ensure that there is no open food or any other items that are a safety concerns such as children or pets (SHUT THEM OUT FOR SAFETY)

If you use household equipment in your manufacturing process, make sure they are used exclusively for that purpose only.

STEEL BUCKET OR SUITABLE LARGER STEEL CONTAINER

For small quantities you can obtain a stainless steel bucket and a thermostatically controlled portable immersion heater, or a 'Baby Burco™' type heated immersion boiler, from hardware supplies or yard sales.   Just ensure that the suitable container is of sufficient size to handlethe quantity required and can stand being heated up whilst manufacturing your biodiesel.

Figure 6

After all, you don't want a container that is too small, which could cause a safety hazard such as spillage or splashing.

When you progress to larger quantities, you can make your own reactor for production using such things as old household water-heater immersion tanks and 40 gallon drums etc, black metal piping and joints, electric pump, and some braided plastic tubing, a few line isolation valves and you're away into a plentiful supply of biodiesel.

We call them 'Apple Seed Reactors'. You will find them on the web.

Professionally built reactors, are sometimes found on eBay, or can be bought on line as can all equipment and supplies needed, and must be thought about seriously if going to produce biodiesel regularly or in bigger quantities to sell on.

The economies of scale then really pay off.

Paying the full price for a new biodiesel reactor or if you prefer processor, really is worthwhile when you consider the many advantages of new versus old equipment. No hassle and equipment has a guarantee. Plus when you make a successful business of it, it becomes tax deductable.

Check out Chapter 11 for deeper insight into Biodiesel Processors/Reactors.

MEASURING CONTAINERS

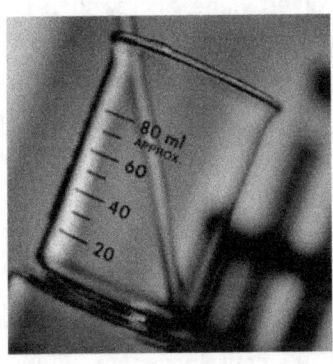

You will need a measuring container in order to measure the amounts of ingredients you need to add to your mixture.

You can purchase measuring containers at any hardware store or store that sells kitchen supplies.

Now don't forget, when measuring lye, you will need to use measuring items that are made out of stainless steel, HDPE, glass or enamel, because the chemicals attack zinc, aluminium, or tin.

NB: It is very important to note that when manufacturing biodiesel, the accuracy of all your measurements is highly important to your results, so the more accurate your equipment the better.

Keep records as you are working; especially write down every small measurement when performing your titrations and you will be on the road to success.

HDPE CONTAINERS

HDPE (High-Density Polyethylene) is a special plastic suitable for mixing your chemicals, and is what you will need in order to make the methoxide.

When you select the container, make sure it is big enough for the amount of mixture you will be adding, and ensure it has a tight stopper and screw on cap to make the process of creating methoxide as safe as possible.

If you do not use an HDPE container, you could also use glass, stainless steel or enamel. Remember, when using lye, you can't just use any container, because lye (caustic soda) reacts with zinc, tin and aluminium.

You can purchase HDPE containers at most hardware stores and do get them with good screw lids and bungs for piercing suction pipes through, and perhaps a special screw cap with tap. HDPE plastics are characterized by the symbol below:

This symbol was created by the American Plastics Council, and indicates that plastics, which carry this symbol, are safe to use with household and industrial chemicals.

Temperature Gauge

See figure 11, page 150

A temperature gauge is required to test the temperature of the oil to make sure that it is not too cool thus giving a poor reaction, and not too hot so that it evaporates the methanol once it is added.

The boiling temperature for methanol is 148.5° F [64.7° C]). You can purchase a temperature gauge from suitable suppliers or from department stores such as Wal-Mart™ or Tesco™ etc.

In fact a temperature gauge used in motor vehicles is about right because you need relatively low readings when making biodiesel. I would say you need to heat your oil to around 120° to 130° Fahrenheit or 48° to 54° Centigrade.

Stirring Mechanism

Once the methoxide is added to the heated oil, the mixture then needs to be stirred continuously for two hours otherwise a complete chemical reaction will not happen. Due to the fact that this is a dangerous process, you must wear protective gloves at all times.

Therefore, when you don't have the machine processors to produce biodiesel like a laboratory in a large plant, you need to improvise. What many people do is to use a power drill held in a jig, and fit a paint stirrer to the end of the drill. Experiment stirring water to find the correct speed. Many find this gets the job done without causing splashing.

SEPARATION OF BIODIESEL & GLYCERINE

How to separate biodiesel from the glycerine?

Once the process is complete and your biodiesel has been left to settle for 8 hours, you will need a pump to remove the biodiesel from the glycerine. You don't have to spend a lot of money to obtain a siphon. Siphon pumps used for cleaning fish tanks will work just fine for small quantities and can be purchased at a pet store. When dealing with larger quantities you can either have a 'bottom drain' in the larger containers or use a mechanical pump to remove glycerine from base.

WARNING: Never siphon off the glycerine as in the 'petrol tank' method.

i.e. never use your mouth for this as Methanol & Methoxide (Methyl ester) can kill you!

OTHER EQUIPMENT

Other equipment that you may wish to purchase, if making biodiesel becomes your new hobby, includes in no particular order:

- Reactor/processor

- Pump

- Filters

- Titration kits, glass calibrated beaker, pipette (eye dropper) calibrated in millilitres, 10/5/2 ml oral syringes calibrated in millilitres etc

- Phenolphthalein – indicator (not 'Universal Indicator')

- Biodiesel reactor parts

- Heaters

- Wash tank

- Litmus sticks or papers

- Refractometers, pH meter, Viscosity meters and more.

SAFETY CLOTHING AND EQUIPMENT

You can buy biodiesel equipment online from a number of retailers

Check - 'Resources'

Safety Clothing Equipment

The essential safety equipment that you should use when making biodiesel is as follows:

- Chemical proof safety goggles or full face mask

- Chemical proof gloves

- Respirators suitable for working with methanol and 'methoxide'.

- Chemical proof apron

- Long pants

- Boots

Some enlightened individuals even go a step by beyond the items listed above, and will even sport a lab coat as well as a full-face shield and respirator. Regardless of what you choose, the important thing is to stay as safe as possible.

This means protecting your skin, eyes, nose and mouth from the harmful vapours of methanol and lye and its mixtures by working outside or in a very well ventilated area.

Just remember to use safe protective clothing and safety gear, simply because you are using potentially dangerous chemicals

When you make biodiesel you will want to keep these things in mind:

Figure 7

Make sure that –

- Keep a very well ventilated area preferably outside.

- Immediate access to running water through a hosepipe with spray nozzle attached. Methanol or methoxide should be washed off immediately for 15 minutes, because it can damage nerves beneath the skin, even unbroken skin before you even notice the burn!

- Eyes should be washed out with copious amounts of running water, paying careful attention to washing under the eye-lids, and then seek urgent medical assistance.

- Never accompanied by children or pets. (Keep them shut out)

- Vinegar – in squeeze bottle to help neutralize spillages of methanol.

- Fire precautions. – Get advice from local fire prevention services.

When it comes to safety and methanol, the other thing you have to keep in mind is that methanol is highly flammable.

Therefore, you should be conscious of where you keep your methanol at all times.

Keep it in a cool, well ventilated place and make sure it is never near any open flame or sparks.

Finally, don't forget that staying safe is about taking precautions and using your common sense.

There is no reason why you should feel panicked or worried about using these chemicals. Knowledge counts as long as you know what you are doing.

By handling the chemicals with care and keeping them sealed and in a safe place when not in use, you should have no problems.

Remember, methanol vapours are at their most dangerous when the chemical is heated; cold methanol gives off extremely low vapours.

METHOD

HOMEMADE STEP-BY-STEP BIODIESEL

PRODUCTION PROCESS FOR S.V.O (STRAIGHT VEGETABLE OIL) ONLY

All right, so now you know everything you need in order to make this homemade biodiesel recipe and in safety. That means there is only one thing left to do – it's time to show you how it's done!

STEP 1 – MAKING METHOXIDE (SODIUM HYDROXIDE SOLUTION IN METHANOL) S.V.O ONLY

After setting up all your equipment, and decking yourself out in all your safety gear, it's time to begin the first step of the process, which involves making the amount of methoxide needed to produce 10 litres of biodiesel from S.V.O

Measure out your 2 litres of methanol and carefully add it to your ample sized HDPE plastic container a little at a time so as not to cause splashing.

Then mix the 3.5 grams of lye per litre of vegetable oil = 3.5 X 10 = 35 grams of lye into the methanol (a little at a time). Once everything is added, replace the stopper and lid. With the lid on tight keep swirling the mixture around for 10 minutes or so, and then let it stand.

You will notice that when you mix these two chemicals together, a reaction will occur almost instantly, which is known as exothermic reaction that generates heat.

All in all this process should take about 15 minutes to fully mix for this recipe (The advantage of using HDPE is that you can see if all the lye has dissolved – make sure it has).

(Note: large quantities of lye and methanol should not be mixed by using the method above, and should be mixed with proper, safer equipment.

Furthermore, larger batches can take more than 24 hours to thoroughly dissolve)

Step 2 – Warming the S.V.O (straight vegetable oil)

Add the 10* litres of new vegetable oil to the stainless steel or other suitable container and warm your oil 120° to 130° Fahrenheit or 48° to 54° Celsius.

Please make sure before you start that there is enough room for both the vegetable oil and the methoxide mixture with room to spare.

This process will help to thin out the oil so that when it comes time for it to mix with the methoxide it will blend better.

Just make sure that you don't let the oil get too hot; stay around 120° to 130° Fahrenheit maximum, which equals 48° to 54° Celsius maximum, because if too hot, the methanol will evaporate and spoil your biodiesel production.

(Keep in mind: the boiling temperature for methanol is 148.5° F [64.7° C]). See figure 11.

Step 3 – Add 2* litres premixed Methoxide (equals 20% of vegetable oil used) + Lye to the heated oil

When the methoxide mixture is ready and the oil is at the proper temperature, carefully add the methoxide to the oil whilst outside, if not using an immersion heater.

Stir well, firmly but gently, so not to spill using "stirring mechanism" if available. A reaction starts immediately.

Keeping the liquid heated between 120° to 130°F / 48° to 54°C. Continue to stir the mixture for two hours (very important) before letting it stand. This is the crucial time. Temperature and constant stirring are a must for those vital first two important hours.

STEP 4 – LET MIXTURE SETTLE

After the stirring is complete, let the mixture settle, gradually brown fluid (glycerine) will settle on the bottom and a clear "candle wax to a golden-amber colour" liquid (biodiesel) will surface on top.

(IMPORTANT: Settle for a Minimum of 8 hours but up to 24 hours preferably)

NB: * - Small test batches just scale down the amounts.

STEP 5 – REMOVE BIODIESEL

The following day it's time to see if you were successful at making biodiesel. Take your pump and remove the glycerine from bottom.

(Danger! - NEVER suck out the glycerine with a piece of tubing to your mouth in the "Petrol Tank" fashion, the methoxide could kill you).

When all is said and done you should have 10 litres of biodiesel and a leftover of 2 litres of raw glycerine in the bottom of the container.

The final product before separation should look something like this photograph. The darker bottom of the measure is the glycerine, and the clear amber-yellowish liquid above is the biodiesel.

How Your Biodiesel Should Look Before Separation from the Glycerine

Figure 8

There you have it – That was the crude old way they made biodiesel, now let us see the correct safer way of making your biodiesel. So stay safe and make the most of your biodiesel adventure! Enjoy cost-effective, eco magnificent, motoring miles.

Diagrammatic Illustration of

Merv's Step-By-Step Biodiesel Production Process

(This diagram is for understanding the process only and not recommended)

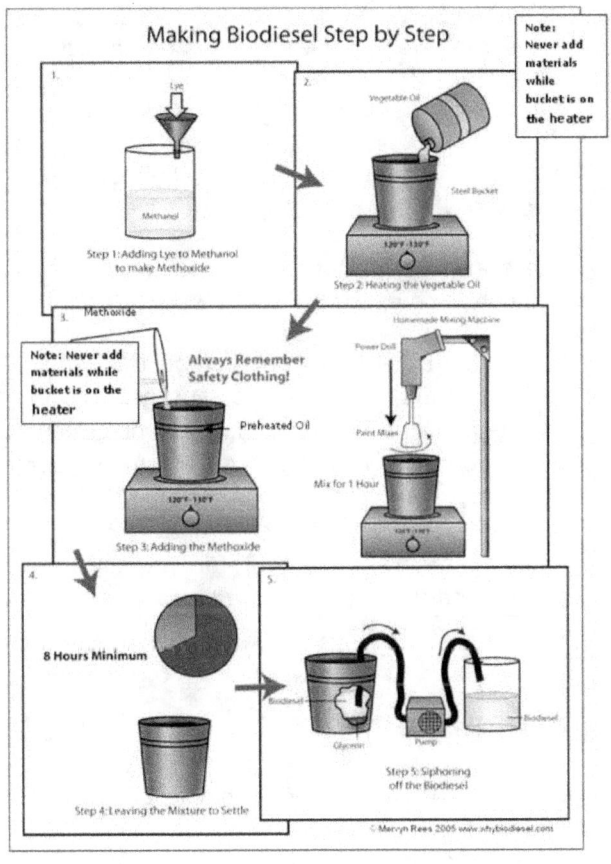

Figure 9

Caution - Please Read On

Before you rush off to make your first batch of 'home-made biodiesel' may I suggest you read on, for like most seemingly simple ideas, like an iceberg there is much more below the surface than you see above the water, 90% more in fact!

For example you will find that when you get to W.V.O (waste vegetable oil) the art of titration is an entirely different 'ball of wax' and you will discover whole new chemicals and their dangers.

There are many more examples, which of course make it all so exciting.

As you really start to understand this whole new world you are stepping into, and as you gain the knowledge, the fun you have coming your way with your new hobby or perhaps booming business, you will also be aware that you are helping your environment and how you are enjoying the rewards of it for yourself and your family, and that's just for starters.

Storing Biodiesel

When it comes to storing biodiesel you will find that it is a fairly simple process, as biodiesel can be stored wherever crude oil based diesel is stored, with the exception of concrete-lined tanks.

You shouldn't store biodiesel for longer than a year, as the fuel quality is known to disintegrate over time as it does all petro-fuels (fossil fuels) also.

Furthermore, biodiesel should not be stored in cold temperatures as this also has negative effects on renewable fuel.

Some manufactures put vitamin E into their fuel as an anti-oxidant.

You can learn more about the shelf life and cold store properties in the "Drawbacks" section in Chapter 6.

TITRATION BY NUMBERS

This section is a must for W.V.O (waste vegetable oil).

When performing a 'Titration' we will come up with results that give a particular number, from 0 to 9, (these numbers are known as acid numbers).

We take our resulting number and then we will work out how many grams of lye over the base amount we will need (base being 3.5 grams of NaOH (lye) per 1-litre of oil used).

Let us say we get a '2' result, this equals a 2-ml titration which tells us to add an extra 2 grams of lye for each 1- litre of oil you are actually using to make your biodiesel, and so on pro-rata, this compensates for the side reaction caused by the FFA's (free fatty acids) unique to this particular batch of oil.

Once any vegetable oil has been used it must by its very nature undergo a chemical change caused by the amount and extent of heat used and the various mixtures of material cooked within it, plus the waste materials left behind.

All these factors are what make each new batch of waste oil unique, and that is why it is imperative to carry out a new titration every single time.

LET'S PLAY! - - For the Titration you will require:

One Scale– versatile, perhaps something smaller from science supply houses, eBay, second-hand goods stores or yard sales as long as it is sensitive to weighing small amounts and accurate.

One pack of lye – NaOH (caustic soda) from hardware store or **KOH- (Red Devil™ lye)** – from internet.

One bottle of phenolphthalein or phenol red indicator. Generally pool suppliers have phenol red. Whereas phenolphthalein is generally sold at, wine makers, lab-supply-houses or science-educational-suppliers, check the internet.

One isopropyl alcohol – at least 90% proof isopropyl (rubbing alcohol) or as an example 99% proof red bottle IsoHeet™ from auto parts stores

Three oral 10ml syringes – graduated in millilitres – from drug stores.

One bottle of distilled water preferably but de-ionized will do.

One empty bottle to store 1 litre of the lye water.

One measuring device – measurer – 1 litre graduated cylinders, or a large kitchen measure jug.

Four or five small beakers or jars – to use as the titration 'beaker', for sample of oil, and for handling the 0.1% NaOH solution to avoid the syringe contaminating the whole bottle of lye water.

One pack litmus test sticks/papers – pH indicator.

If serious amounts of biodiesel are to be made, then you could consider a pH meter.

Rag or wipes to wipe out the 'beaker' between titrations.

Of course, do not forget, your supply of S.V.O or your W.V.O.

The chemistry of biodiesel is simple but to get constant good results your bi-word has to be accuracy. Another good tip is to take notice when you are using your 'oral' syringe, you will see the fluid in the glass or plastic as curved instead of a straight line. Don't worry; just use the bottom of the curve from where you measure.

Step 1.

Lye-Water – Reference Tester

Solution

To make a 0.1% NaOH in distilled water solution, use 1 gram of catalyst (lye or KOH) dissolved in 1 litre of distilled water.

This is a mixture of 1/1000. If you find this measuring too difficult then use 5 grams in 5 litres of distilled water, same result.

You now have your lye-water for testing.

Never test from it, always pour a small sample into another container for your actual test, this way you will never contaminate your master testing material.

Step 2.

How to make a blank titration

Sometimes alcohol becomes slightly acidic with age, which would throw off your results. Therefore, test it by performing a blank titration periodically.

A blank titration looks just like a regular titration but without the oil. A blank titration neutralizes any acids that the isopropyl contained, so you are starting with a 'blank' slate and your real titration only reads the free fatty acids instead of the acids in the isopropyl.

Step 3.

Isopropyl

- Also known as 1-methylethyl (<u>IUPAC</u>)

Add 10 ml of isopropyl to your 'beaker'

Step 4.

Phenolphthalein is a <u>pH indicator</u> used for <u>acid-base titrations</u>, which turns pink when right pH achieved.

We are looking to achieve optimal pH = 7 (neutral).

Add 4 or 5 drops of phenolphthalein or phenol red into the beaker with the isopropyl in it.

Step 5.

Gently swirl contents.

It will change to a yellowish colour.

Step 6.

Now, add lye-water drop by drop and keep swirling.

Important: Count the drops added, check readings on syringe, before and after titration. Pay attention to accurate measurements. Keep records whenever you measure – at all times.

The moment it turns pink/red – Stop

Well done, you have neutralized all the acids in the isopropyl.   This is your starting point. (Congratulations – You have just performed your first blank titration)

You will now proceed to add an exact 1-ml measure of your oil to this mixture for the actual titration step. ***Swirl your** beaker etc (see step 7)

There are cases where it takes only a few drops to of lye water to neutralize the acids, and some say don't bother with it unless you require at least half a millilitre of lye-water with these titrations with this particular isopropyl – low acidic, and all that.

I would say perform a blank titration each time, it only takes 30 seconds or so when you are used to it, so why not?

We need to be accurate, so always perform a real titration for a neutral starting point for constant good results!

Step 7.

Accurate   Measurement   of   Sample
Using your oral syringes and using a separate
syringe for each fluid, carefully measure 10 ml of
isopropyl alcohol into your beaker, now add an
exact 1-ml measure of your oil.   This oil
measurement has to be very accurate.

Never try to suck up just the amount of material
you need, always a lot more than needed and then
the empty fluids back until you have the correct
measure. If you did not do a blank titration add 5
drops of phenolphthalein or phenol red pH
indicator, or you can measure right into the same
liquids as you did the blank titration on. ***Swirl
your** beaker to mix and liquid, which will turn
yellow after you have added the oil.

Make sure your oil is very fluid, warm if necessary,
otherwise you will have blobbing problems, you
don't want it to form big bubbles of oil.   Keep
swirling while doing the next few steps to keep
these blobs from forming. You can now see the oil
properly suspended in the isopropyl.

Step 8.

Adding Lye-Water Solution & Measuring

Now, into your beaker add the lye-water solution a drop at a time, and keep track of how much you're adding, (it's important for calculating amount of lye needed). Keep swirling your fluid, until it turns the beaker contents a pink/red colour that lasts for 30 seconds or longer, depending on product used.

Remember; do not mix up your syringes, (or eye-dropper). Each fluid must have its own syringe; clean them with your isopropyl alcohol if you make a mistake.

Phenol red and phenolphthalein will stay red/pink for different amounts of time. The phenol red will usually turn back to yellow after a half minute or so, but the phenolphthalein will stay pink.

Step 9.

Check Lye-Water amount.

This is when your lye-water neutralizes the FFA's (free fatty acids).

How much lye-water is used?

Every 1ml of lye-water equals an extra 1gram of lye that you have to add to make your 1liter quantity; this neutralizes the free fatty acids in this oil.

If your oil takes more than 4 ml of lye, more for KOH, best not use this oil until you are more experienced. Normally 'fast food' oil will need 2 or 3 ml for the titration.

NB – Titration – You must use same lye source you are using for making your biodiesel. Whatever lye you choose to use in your lye-water you must use the same lye all way through to the final product.

Step 10a (Using NaOH).

This section is for NaOH only.

Normal useable quantities for biodiesel manufacturing

So now, you know how much lye to use in every 1-litre of oil you have to make your diesel.

OK your biodiesel processor/reactor is ready and waiting – time to get stuck in!

Remember to calibrate your processor in litres, so you can tell at a glance how many litres you are working with. To find out how much catalyst (lye) to use, you will multiply the following:

Using NaOH

Number of litres of oil x (3.5 grams Lye (NaOH) plus titration results)

Example for NaOH

If titration showed 3 ml, then I add 3 extra grams of lye over base, for every litre of oil I am going to use in my processor. If I am processing 120 litres of oil, I do the simple sums:

120 litres oil x (3.5 grams Lye (NaOH) + 3 grams extra Lye) = 780

same as

120 litres oil x 6.5 grams NaOH (lye) = 780 grams NaOH

same as

120 x 6.5 = 780 grams of NaOH (lye) for this particular batch of oil to be processed.

Step 10b (Using KOH).

This section is for KOH only.

Using KOH

In the same way for KOH as for NaOH (lye). There is a slight difference in the results using KOH-water when performing your titration. However, exactly in the same way, use whatever acid-number is shown. The main difference is in the base numbers, because KOH has a base number of 5 grams per litre, as against the base number of NaOH, which as you know, is 3.5 grams per litre. So if this KOH-water titration requires 3ml for this oil that gives us a value of an extra 3 grams per every 1litre of oil, then follow below.

Example for KOH:

120-litre oil in processor, times KOH (lye) catalyst, plus titration, which showed 3 ml for that oil = 3 grams extra KOH (lye)

Same as

120 x (5 grams KOH (lye) + 3 grams KOH) = 960 grams KOH

Same as

120 x 8 = 960 grams of KOH (lye) for this particular batch of oil to be processed.

Some find KOH troublesome because it has various grades proof. You need at least 85% proof, but I think best to use the 99% proof, otherwise you have to keep working out how much more to add for the lower grades.

There will be no need to alter titration results because it will still automatically show up the correct levels.

How to make your own biodiesel

Now that you know the basic gist of the process that is involved in the creation of biodiesel, this next section has been created to provide you with information on how you can produce your own homemade biodiesel, through a basic recipe.

In addition, don't worry even if chemistry wasn't your forte when you went to school. You should find the step-by-step instructions quite easy to follow.

Warning – Take care to check out and pay attention to all safety aspects of working with chemicals especially when making your own biodiesel.

Read "Safety Clothing Equipment" (Chapter 3, Page 78)

WARNING – The author of this book assumes no responsibilities for any actions you take resulting from the following information provided about making biodiesel.

The chemical ingredients, methanol, sodium hydroxide and potassium hydroxide are dangerous, poisonous chemicals that can cause serious physical harm and even death.

You are responsible for your own actions, as well as the safety of yourself and others around you including your pets.

WHERE TO BEGIN

First things first, you need acquire all of the ingredients and equipment you will need to make your first batch of biodiesel.

Therefore, before you obtain the ingredients, you need to decide on whether or not you will be making biodiesel from new vegetable oil (S.V.O) or waste vegetable oil (W.V.O) and which 'lye' you are going to use.

For 'Merv's Thermometer for Biodieselers' please check out Fig 10.

©MERV'S THERMOMETER FOR BIODIESELERS

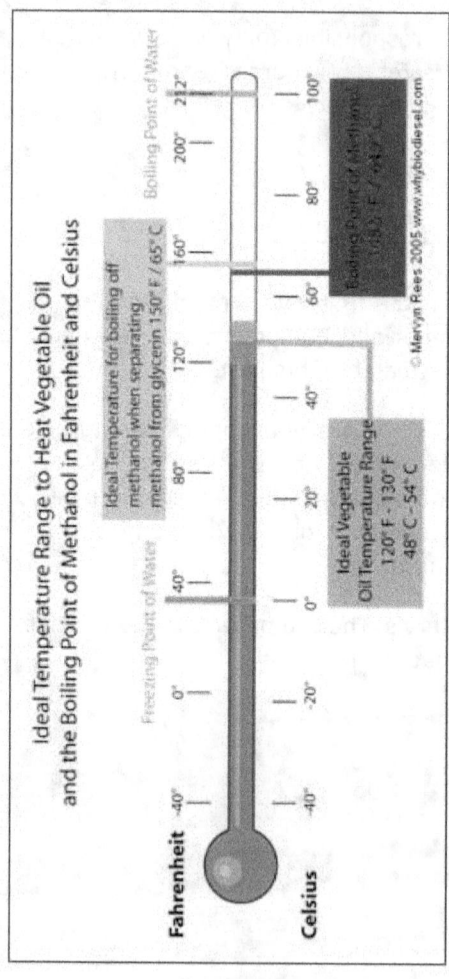

Figure 10

RECIPE 1. - S.V.O.

FOR TURNING S.V.O (STRAIGHT VEGETABLE OIL) INTO BIODIESEL

Ingredients: To make 10 litres of Biodiesel

- 10 litres of any new vegetable oil

- 2 litres of methanol alcohol (CH_3OH) (99% + pure)

- Prepare the methoxide (methyl ester)

- 35 grams of lye using (NaOH) (sodium hydroxide) (caustic soda)

- {Or 50 grams of lye – if using lye from using 99% proof (KOH)}

Check oil and heat to correct temperature, see gauge above.

Add methoxide in correct manner safely.

Stir continuously for 2 hours at correct temperature.

Allow this mixture to settle for at least 8 hours preferably up to 24 hours.

Once settled, remove the glycerine.

Wash, dry & filter to 3 microns at least but to 1 micron for top biodiesel.

Details of the above working of this recipe will be found on other pages.

Check the quality visually for a clear translucency (see page 28).

RECIPE 2. - W.V.O.

PROCEDURE WHEN USING W.V.O.
(WASTE VEGETABLE OIL)

Same as for S.V.O but will have to add extra lye per litre for W.V.O to compensate for free fatty acids according to amount of use had.

The extra problems using W.V.O are removing the many contaminants that cooking brings, (seen & unseen). On the plus side you will mostly get your supplies free. So more work, but more profit if it is done correctly.

Filter the waste vegetable oil (W.V.O.) in order to remove any solid pieces and food scraps.

Pre-Heat the W.V.O. to remove by evaporation any potential water content.

Gather titration ingredients & kit together:

- Isopropyl alcohol (rubbing alcohol) (99% + pure)

- Distilled water or de-ionized water to make lye water tester.

- Phenolphthalein solution – acid based indicator.

- Sample of oil

- Litmus sticks/papers or PH digital Meter.

- Beakers & mixing rods

- Syringes

- Suitable protective gloves etc see 'Safety Clothing & Equipment'.

Perform titration to gauge the amount of required catalyst.

Make up methoxide in correct safety manner

Add methoxide in correct safety manner to W.V.O. at correct temperature

Stir mixture continuously for 2 hours at correct temperature.

Allow this mixture to settle for 8 hours minimum preferably 24 hours.

Separate biodiesel from glycerine

Wash, dry & filter to 3 microns at least but to 1 micron or top biodiesel.

Details of the working of this recipe will be found on other pages.

Check the quality visually for a clear translucency (see Fig 8 on page 85).

How Do You Wash Biodiesel?

What is 'Washing' Biodiesel?

Washing Methods most used.

1. Mist Washing

2. Bubble Washing

3. Stir Washing

4. Dry Washing

Before biodiesel is ready for use, all quality biodiesel, whether it is made using S.V.O or W.V.O, must first be washed so that all of the leftover contaminants can be removed from it.

Washing biodiesel involves passing water through the newly formed biodiesel in very fine droplets, so gathering all surplus particles of lye, methanol, metal, sulphur, chlorophyll, free glycerine,

glycerine, soaps and other waste matter as it falls through to the bottom of the reactor/processor.

However before I proceed, I must mention that some people believe that biodiesel does not need to be washed, because they think that the remaining lye, methanol, metal, sulphur, chlorophyll, free glycerine, glycerine, soaps, other contaminants etc., will not do enough harm to bother.

They do not believe these leftovers will damage their engine. Wrong!

Well I can tell you that it is common to find unwashed biodiesel in all sorts of equipment and vehicles, mostly heavy commercial, tractors, farm equipment, generators and the like, and yes, some use it straight into their trucks and vans. If one of these vehicles should go by, you will always know because you will get the different aromas, such as 'burgers & fries' etc. Does it do harm – YES – but some say, well it depends how you look at it.

The superior lubricity of biodiesel certainly compensates for a lot! Yes but if you have a more modern sophisticated diesel vehicle, with the management systems typical today and expensive high performance injectors needing top fuel to perform, then simply don't do it!

Do not use unfiltered and unwashed biodiesel in your vehicle!

Now where was I?

Washing is necessary to remove remaining contaminants from the biodiesel before it is used. This includes elements that would clog injectors, chemicals which produce noxious substances after combustion.

If you have used W.V.O to make your biodiesel, there will obviously be extra contaminants involved from the cooking it was used for previously, but S.V.O also needs washing. It is obviously cleaner, but then that's why we use less lye when manufacturing. But never the less there are still contaminants besides residual lye and methanol that can be removed.

There are various methods of washing, below is a brief overview:

Mist Washing

Commonly known as cleaning through the "waterfall effect", this involves a fine spray of water onto the surface of the processed fuel. The small water droplets falling through the biodiesel gather the impurities out of the fuel. This involves no agitation of the processed fuel, therefore very forgiving of a possible high soap factor in the final fuel and avoids forming an emulsion during the washing process. It is important to remember, however, that a well-processed, good quality fuel is resistant to forming an emulsion at this stage anyway.

Mist washing is slow, and uses a large quantity of water which is unsuitable for recycling after use, but it is generally the most often used way at present.

Bubble washing

To bubble wash, a different sequence of wash steps is involved, each of which involves adding clean water (approximately a quarter of the volume of the fuel mix is normal). The water will sink to the bottom of the container and stay separate from the fuel. An aquarium pump (or similar) is used at the bottom of the reactor/processor to blow air up through the water. This means that the air forms bubbles, and the bubbles have a skin of water – as this passes up through the fuel, it cleans it.

When the bubble reaches the surface it bursts, and the water re-sinks to the bottom of the container again this time taking more impurities with it. Once the washing period is complete, the container is left to settle (for at least an hour, probably better longer), until it is clearly separated. The water is now drained from the processor using a bottom mounted tap.

This process is repeated until the water drained has a pH of 7, meaning that most impurities have been removed from the fuel and signifying that the fuel is now washed. Wash periods are usually around 4 hours each, though the initial period can be shorter.

Obviously, this method involves some agitation of the mix, but it is still considered a "gentle" wash method, and is therefore also considered forgiving of poor quality fuels.

A serious disadvantage to bubble washing is the danger of oxidization. By bubbling air through the fuel, the oil in it can be oxidized. This can cause a build-up of hard plastic-like deposits in a fuel system, which is ironically exactly what washing is supposed to avoid! Because of this, I personally prefer mist washing to bubble washing. The chances of oxidization vary according to the types of oil in use and the pressure from the airbrick. Potentially this may not be a problem if using S.V.O, whereas with W.V.O. the exact oils in use may not be known, making control even more difficult.

One important thing to note about bubble washing is that the output and any hose of the pump in use WILL be exposed to the methanol you are trying to wash out so it must not be made of a perishable material.

Stir Washing

Remembering that the above gentler washes are forgiving of poor quality fuel mixes because they did not agitate the mix much or at all, it should be quite clear that stir washing is going to be more demanding of the quality of the fuel mix produced. So experiment on a small sample first.

Stir washing consists of adding water to the fuel container, and stirring thoroughly until the water and fuel form a single consistent liquid. This liquid is then left to settle, the water drained off, and the process repeated until the drained water has a pH7.

This method is much faster than the previous two (meaning hours to complete rather than days!), but beware, it is absolutely unforgiving of poor quality fuel mixes. Poorly made biodiesel will simply produce an emulsion and refuse to separate after being stirred, and your batch of fuel mix will be ruined.

NB: It is important to realize that the method for testing the quality of any biodiesel after production is to add water to a sample and SHAKE until mixed, and then leave to settle. High quality biodiesel will separate quickly and cleanly.

So in conclusion stir-wash test samples of all the biodiesel that you produce!

Dry Washing of Biodiesel

Dry means dry, ergo we do not use any water!

This new and exciting development in the evolution of biodiesel manufacturing is rapidly improving both the quality and the time taken in making biodiesel to the very highest of standards.

Organizations worldwide have variations in standards set at the moment, from ASTM D6751 for FAMAE in USA, in Germany provisional specification for FAME that is DIN V 51606, and the UK/Europe with Europe's Committee for Standardization ("CEN") technical standard for biofuels known as EN 14214-2005 applies to FAME.

This European standard is very stringent with tight limits on sulphur and water as well as the oxidation stability.

These last three requirements are not in the STM Specification at the time of writing.

Q. So, what is this magical development?

Getting rid of the water wash cycle!

This is how it works. A powder in the form of a very active 'Synthetic Magnesium Silicate Absorbent' trademarked by the Dallas Group of America Inc., and registered as Magnesol® does the washing instead of water.

When this man-made version of synthetic magnesium silicate is used as an absorbent filter aid, being very active, it takes up and holds the various potential contaminants. These are metals, sulphur, plus chlorophyll, soaps, fatty acids, methanol, free glycerine, glycerine, colourings, odour or water that are found in bio diesels and are then easily filtered out.

It is said that if another magnesium silicate-like talcum powder were used, it would not work because mined magnesium silicate in the raw state is 'inactive' in the main.

Magnesol® is widely in use already in the catering world across North America and elsewhere.

As I understand it, it has greatly extended the working life of the cooking oils in industry and restaurants.

Well how do you use Magnesol® in biodiesel production?

For a 'dry' wash of biodiesel, you simply eliminate the water washing cycle in the production line. After the removal of methanol and the glycerine produced in the 'transesterification' process, you eliminate the water washing all together, and all that needs to happen is a mixing of the Magnesol® with the unwashed separated biodiesel for a period of 20 minutes.

The magnesium silicate attracts the polar compound (contaminants) which are then removed by filtration.

These contaminants are now in the form of a 'cake' rather than effluent, and therefore easily manageable.

Research into the uses for this by-product is ongoing, apart from being a compost viable material; they are looking at this as a biomass-fuel, among other things.

Q. Is Magnesol® a Safe Chemical?
Source: Dallas Group of America Inc.

If swallowed or inhaled drink water and/or blow your nose.

Accidental Ingestion of this product does not require first aid

Wash skin thoroughly with soap and water.

Eyes – Flush out eyes with plenty of water. Call your doctor if irritation persists.

Q. What does it cost?

Like all things it would appear to be the economy of scale, and will depend upon the quality of your biodiesel. Costs are reported to be in the order of 1 to 10 US cents per gallon.

Q. Do I need a fancy filter?

No – only a low-tech filter is required.

Usually down to 3 Microns (down to 1 Micron for top end product).

Therefore, the benefits of using this 'Dry Wash' are:

1. No water effluent

2. No emulsification

3. Improved oxidative stability

4. Cost effective

5. Time saving

6. Very forgiving in cleaning up your work.

Q. What happens if I want to do a regular water wash with my biodiesel, and then use this Magnesol® or similar product dry method?

Well obviously, nothing that did not happen before, except you will now be polishing up your biodiesel to a much better standard and, if done properly, achieving the high standards we all desire.

Of course, it will take that much longer.

A lot of 'biodieselers' are in fact doing just that.

There are filtering systems available that allow filtering down to 1-Micron.

However, there is claimed to be an increased efficacy 'dry washing' without the water wash.

Conclusion - To each their own!

Q. Are there any other manufacturers of a dry wash filtering materials like Magnesol®?

Yes there are, Biodys Engineering in Holland for example, provide its own brand called Magnidon™.

It is a magnesium silicate enriched with bleaching earth powder and was specially developed for waterless biodiesel cleaning. It is a very cost effective and time saving product.

See resource page.

There may well be others as I have seen articles by chemical manufacturers in China & India.

Chapter 4

Glycerine

Glycerine (glycerol) is the primary by-product that comes from making biodiesel. However, so as not to create any confusion, the glycerine that is produced from biodiesel is not the same as pure glycerine, which is a non-toxic, viscous liquid that is odourless, colourless and tastes very sweet.

Pure glycerine has thousands of uses, and should not be mistaken with the biodiesel by-product known as crude glycerine that will be discussed in this chapter.

The glycerine produced when making biodiesel is crude, a light to medium brown, and it not only is comprised of glycerine, it also contains excess methanol, lye and soap etc.

Therefore, if you wish to do something with the glycerine aside from chucking it out, you will first need to separate it from the other products within it.

Keep in mind that while you can actually sell glycerine that has been properly separated. It is usually only sold by the ton, so selling small amounts is more trouble than the process is worth.

Nevertheless, even if it is not your plan to sell it, there are a few other things you can use it for.

Therefore, the next section provides you with basic details of what's involved in order to separate glycerine.

Separating Glycerine

First of all, the information below has not been created as instructions for you to follow on how to separate glycerine.

The separation of glycerine can be a tedious process that takes skill.

Most of the methanol used in making your biodiesel ends up in the glycerine.

So what you can do is pre-form a coil of copper tubing, making a distillation mechanism from the top of your reactor and have the tubing going back down into a suitable sealed container to receive the distilled methanol for reuse by heating your glycerine to 150°F/66°C which is just above methanol's boiling point.

In order to separate glycerine from the lye, soap and methanol traces, you'll need to use concentrated phosphoric acid ($H3PO4$), which is 85% strength. The remaining 15% is primarily water. Furthermore, phosphoric acid is corrosive chemical, so take care if, or when, you decide to use it.

The amount of phosphoric acid you will need is roughly 1.5 – 1.7ml x the amount of each gram of lye you used when making biodiesel.

Thus, since it is about 3.5 grams of lye that is used per litre of straight vegetable oil, and let us say there are 2 litres, then that would be 3.5 x 2 = 7.0 grams of lye.

Multiply that by the phosphoric acid, and you would need between 8.25 – 9.35 ml.

However, keep in mind that this amount will change based on whether or not you are extracting glycerine produced from S.V.O or W.V.O based biodiesel.

Remember, W.V.O originally contained FFA, which means on top of the ideal lye amount needed per litre (3.5 grams) you also have to take into account the amount you used during titration to create the catalyst that would effectively neutralize the FFA in the oil.

To begin with, you'll first have to siphon or drain the biodiesel before you do anything.

Once the biodiesel is removed you can begin the separation process by adding the right amount of phosphoric acid to the layer of glycerine and mix well.

A reaction will occur that will likely produce heat, as the phosphoric acid works to convert soap back to FFA, and separate it from the glycerine and lye.

As you continue to stir, you will eventually begin to see a translucent yellow layer of glycerine float to the top, leaving behind a dark layer of FFA, and finally the left over catalyst, which is a yellowy colour.

When the process is complete, the FFA will be on the surface, the glycerine – methanol – water mixture in the middle and the leftovers on the bottom. The final result is an estimated product of 90 – 95% pure glycerine, which is good enough for retail purposes.

The amount of glycerine you will gain when separating it will depend upon the amount of biodiesel you've made.

As a general rule of thumb, it is approximated that per litre of oil, there is 79 millilitres of glycerine. Thus, if you have 10 litres of oil, you'll end up with roughly 790 ml of glycerine.

(**Note:** when the biodiesel process is complete, the remaining mixture contains FFA, even if the biodiesel was produced using new oil. Don't forget in order to make biodiesel you had to first heat the oil, and once oil is heated, FFA's form.)

How to dispose of glycerine

Aside from just tossing it in the trash, there are different ways by which you can dispose of glycerine, if you don't wish to separate it from the other leftover components.

Burning

You can burn glycerine; however, you should be aware that if the temperature exceeds a certain heat, glycerine could release toxic fumes, which are known as acrolein fumes.

Therefore, if you do decide to burn it, you cannot ensure that the temperature is lower than 392° F (200° C), as the toxic fumes usually release when the temperature is in between 392° F and 572° F (200° C - 300° C) – So don't do it!

Some home-made producers of biodiesel have burned glycerine for the purpose of pre-heating the oil for biodiesel production, a dangerous practice.

Composting

You can always resort to composting any glycerine you have left over, or even glycerine that results from failed batches of biodiesel.

Glycerine biodegrades quickly when there is a big enough compost pile and natural materials are mixed with it.

Thus, in order for glycerine to breakdown, it requires oxygen, and since glycerine is a sticky mass of goop, it needs to be mixed with straw, wood chips, dry leaves and so on, in order for oxygen to reach it.

Furthermore, like all compost, you need to frequently mix all of the materials within it for the glycerine to breakdown.

A word to the wise, you don't want your compost to become too dry, because it needs moisture to break it down.

However, you also don't want it to be too wet because it could cause leaks, and seep out on to your neighbour's yard and attract attention you don't want, such as the neighbour's dog (dogs love grease) or a nervous neighbour informing the EPA of your actions, etc.

Thus, make sure you know what you are getting into, and learn everything you can about proper composting before you use it as an alternative.

How to make use of pure glycerine?

Pure forms of glycerine (not the leftover by-product of biodiesel) can be used for a number of interesting projects. For instance glycerine has been used as:

Food sweetener: Glycerine is a sugar alcohol and is used in the food industry as a sweetener to create foods for people who need to control or can't have sugar, such as diabetics.

Health Drugs: Athletes can take glycerine-based health supplements that are believed to help them perform better in hot temperatures, because the glycerine increases their temperature regulation and blood volume.

Preserving Plants: Glycerine can help preserve foliage (not flowers). It is recommended that an inch should be cut off the stem of the foliage, and then transported to a pot or vase that contains 75% water and 25% glycerine.

Some other uses

Glycerine is also found in other products such as:

- Makeup

- Skin moisturizers

- Toothpaste

- Cakes/desserts

- Manufacturing of paper

- Plastics

- Textiles

- Printing ink

How to make soap

 Soap is the most popular way to re-use glycerine, and it is highly effective, as it moisturizes and makes for a strong degreaser. In order to make soap, you will need to separate the glycerine from the lye, methanol and FFA, and gently boil off the methanol. If you choose to boil off the methanol,

(150°F /66°C) make sure you do not do it over an open flame, and ensure that you wear proper safety gear so as not to inhale any fumes.

Whilst it is still warm and viscous add approximately 5% of essential oils to personal preference, and allow it to stand in an open container for 10 days. You should always do a very careful skin test to check for sensitivity.

Once you have really refined the glycerine, you can

add it to plain liquid soap to create a power-glycerine shampoo, shower/hand soap.

You will find that you don't need to add too much glycerine.

If you have 16 oz /450grams of liquid soap, try adding 3 – 4 oz (85 – 115grams) of glycerine. In addition, make sure you add some of your favourite smelling oils (essential oils) to produce your desired fragrance.

Pure glycerine is soft and gentle with your skin, and is a great way for you to make handmade soaps for yourself, your friends and even to give as gifts.

Imagine, you can make renewable, environmentally friendly fuel for your vehicle, and make nice gifts of handmade soap with the leftovers – what could be better!

This is what we are aiming for, a really clean liquid soap to which we have added some of our very refined glycerine and essential oils.

Never use generally without skin testing for sensitivity.

If you cannot manage good glycerine refinement it will always make good workshop soap until you master the glycerine clean-up!

Chapter 5

The Cost of Making Biodiesel

Before we get to the cost of making biodiesel, it is a good idea first to point out when and why biodiesel production increased to show you how the current cost of production originated.

When did production of biodiesel increase?

In the U.S., the use of biodiesel has dramatically increased over the past several years. Due to this fact, the Energy Conservation Reauthorization Act of 1998 amended the Energy Policy Act, so that it would include biodiesel fuel use as a way to implement federal, state and public service fleets to meet the new alternative fuel use requirements.

Under the Energy Policy Act, pure biodiesel (B100) is recognized as an alternative fuel. However, the more commonly used biodiesel blends of low levels, such as B20, are not recognized as an alternative fuel.

Nevertheless, those fleets that are covered can make a single EPAct credit each time they purchase 450 US gallons of B100, which they can use for B20 blends or higher.

Thus, after the amendment came into place, the number of biodiesel users grew substantially among a variety of organization including the U.S. Postal Service, numerous school districts, national parks, transit authorities, as well as garbage and recycling companies.

They were encouraged to switch to the alternative fuel due to the fact that they could receive a tax credit. This has boosted the production of biodiesel to increase by an estimated 124 million gallons per year.

More information about the tax incentive will be discussed later on in this chapter.

Average plant cost of biodiesel production

The cost of making biodiesel is lower now that it was before.   Part of the reason is that pure biodiesel is recognized as an alternative fuel, so that those who make enough of it can actually apply for a tax return.   In addition, many people are jumping onto the biodiesel band wagon, which means more stations are popping up all over the world, making biodiesel that much more accessible to the average diesel consumer.

To give you a basic idea of how much biodiesel costs per gallon for the average biodiesel producer in the U.S. who publicly sells their fuel, the following is a rundown of the estimated costs at the time of writing, involved in the production of one gallon of biodiesel:

- Oil $0.025 per US gallon.

- Methanol $0.20 per US gallon.

- Labour $0.15 per US gallon.

- Electricity in plant to produce biodiesel $0.10 per US gallon.

- Interest cost to operate plant $0.05 per US gallon.

- Road tax $0.40-60 per US gallon.

- More or less the same in the UK if you swap $ for £'s.

- UK fuel taxes are higher than the States.

- UK Imperial Gallons = 4.546 Litres, US Gallons = 3.7855 Litres.

On average, it may cost a small biodiesel plant that makes one million gallons or less per year, $250,000. This cost is usually lower than a large plant for the reason that small plants produce biodiesel and sell it at the point-of-use. This means that they don't require as many vehicles (if any), because they don't transport their fuel across the country as larger plants do. Thus, in the end, a small plant usually breaks even within a few years of production, whereas it takes longer for a larger plant, which is often why their fuel will cost the consumer more per gallon for their fuel.

Unlike the U.S. biodiesel, fuel produced in some parts of Europe costs less, because no taxes are charged to producers of alternative fuels. This also means they can sell their fuel more cheaply, for a while at least.

Cost of Feedstock

When analyzing the cost of making biodiesel, something else that needs to be considered is the cost of the feedstock.

Feedstock costs make up a large percentage of direct costs in biodiesel production, and include the capital cost and return. Producers can control the cost of feedstock depending on the type of feedstock used. For instance, it takes approximately 7.3 lbs/3.3 Kg of soybean oil, at a cost of $0.20 per lb, to produce one US gallon of biodiesel; the feedstock (oils from seeds etc) cost per US gallon of soy diesel is at least $1.50 at time of writin

However, if the producer chooses to use fats and greases for their feedstock, it is less expensive to make the biodiesel, which can sometimes be as little as *$1.00 per US gallon. And the end result is still the same quality fuel as the soy diesel.

* There are many reasons and conditions that vary the prices quoted for biodiesel and / or the various parts of same. You'll soon spot that no matter where in the world you are, but one thing is for sure, folk do not keep on doing something that does not pay off, and boy, this biodiesel world just keeps on growing!

How much will it cost me to make biodiesel?

At the time of writing, if you choose to make biodiesel yourself, it will cost you an average of about $0.50 - $0.60 per US gallon.

So, if you plan on running your vehicle on biodiesel, it is estimated that the average consumer uses approximately 10 gallons per week, which is roughly 600 gallons per year.

Thus, if you made your own biodiesel it could cost about $360.00 per year to produce 600 US gallons.

Buying biodiesel at the pump

How much would it cost per gallon?

When buying biodiesel at the pump, the price will vary because it all depends on your location and the retailer. However, it is estimated that the cost of buying biodiesel at the pump is from $1.90 - $3.50. Therefore, if the average person uses 600 US gallons per year, that would cost roughly between $1,400 & $2,100 at time of writing.

To give you a better idea of the different ranges in biodiesel prices across the regions of the U.S. Below is a link for biodiesel B20 prices that are generated by the United States Department of Energy where up to date information, can be checked at this URL.
www.eere.energy.gov/afdc

Is it cheaper to buy regular diesel than make my own biodiesel?

Assuming you already have a diesel vehicle, it would be cheaper compared to purchasing fuel, as the average diesel consumer pays over $1.80 per gallon (at time of writing), which is more than $1100 per year. Plus, when you make your own biodiesel you can apply for a tax return.

However, that being said, you have to remember that making your own biodiesel takes work, and you have to devote time to it.

Thus, while making your own biodiesel could put extra money in your pocket, it may not be suitable to your lifestyle, and therefore not worth it in the long run.

How to market surplus biodiesel?

Aside from the cost of making biodiesel, another important cost factor that needs to be taken into account when producing the renewable fuel for commercial sale is marketing. There are different ways in which a company can market surplus biodiesel.

For instance they can:

Make a website

Making a company website is an excellent way to market surplus biodiesel, as well as encouraging people to learn more about the product that is being sold, and why it will benefit them to purchase it.

Furthermore, when companies market online, they open up new possibilities for its organization to get noticed. For instance, they can be added to other biodiesel organization databases free of charge such as the one provided by the NBB at *www.biodiesel.org.*

NBB will include any fuel retailer or distributor in its database as long as its biodiesel meets the ASTM D 6751 standard and offers biodiesel blends of B2 or higher.
www.biodiesel.org/buyingbiodiesel/guide/submit_location.shtm

Sell the biodiesel at point-of use

This will allow for lower costs because the fuel will not need to be transferred to a distant location. Allowing for lower costs generates more sales and gives local consumers more of an incentive to buy.

Make an alliance with another company

Companies producing biodiesel can make a deal with another company that will market and benefit both businesses. For instance, a biodiesel production company can strike up a deal with a local restaurant or food company by using its waste oil for biodiesel production, and in turn provide the other business's transport vehicles with biodiesel fuel. Thus, each company can advertise the benefits it receives from the other.

Innovative Thinking

How one markets surplus biodiesel is all about innovative thinking and knowing everything there is to know about the economy of the area in which one is intending to sell.

The object is to get others involved in the goal by showing consumers how they can benefit from the company and ideas. For instance, take a look at the marketing techniques of the NOCO Energy Corp.

Based in Tonawanda, New York, NOCO Energy Corp was the first company to introduce retail biodiesel in the state of New York in 2003. Now the town of Tonawanda, as well as the Niagara Frontier Transportation Authority, is using vehicles powered by the biodiesel blend B20, provided by NOCO.

In efforts to promote and expand the use of biodiesel, NOCO is working together with the New York State Energy Research and Development Authority (NYSERDA). They hope that with the expansion of biodiesel, farmers will benefit, as their supplies will be needed for production. In addition, NOCO is building a fuelling infrastructure, and is setting up three public pump sites within the Buffalo area that offer alternative fuel. Once construction is complete, the US Postal Service will use the B20 blend offered at these sites.

As you can see, there are many ways in which one can market surplus biodiesel. It is simply a matter of knowledge, how one goes about doing it, and the budget with which one has to work.

Can I sell the biodiesel that I make?

Yes, you are permitted to sell modest quantities (for instance US 2000 gals. per year) of homemade biodiesel for "research purposes". However, if you are interested in selling your biodiesel commercially in the United States, there are certain requirements you must follow such as:

- Your biodiesel will need to meet the ASTM standard ASTM D 6751 (visit Chapter 7 "False and Truths" section for details on the ASTM)

- You will require permits

- You will be required to charge road tax at time of writing

(An estimated cost of US $0.40-$0.60 per gallon).

However, on the up side, if you do sell your own biodiesel commercially, in the US you will be eligible to obtain a tax incentive.

As for regulations for any other country, you will have to check with its government's taxation authorities.

Tax Incentive USA

The biodiesel tax incentive is a federal excise tax credit that officially took place in January 2005, and was to be in effect for two years. Its purpose was to make the cost of biodiesel lower for consumers in both tax exempt and taxable markets, this seems to be a moving target and needs checking.

The relevant IRS forms for biodieselers are available on the Internal Revenue Service's website (*www.irs.gov*), or at your local IRS office, which is also found on the aforementioned US government website.

The way the incentive works, according to the NBB's 'Biodiesel Tax Incentive Facts Sheet', is "credit equates to one penny per percent of biodiesel in a fuel blend made from agricultural products like vegetable oils, and one-half penny per percent for recycled oils.

The incentive is taken at the blender level, meaning petroleum distributors, and passed on to the consumer."

Before the tax incentive in the year 2004, approximately 30 million gallons of biodiesel was sold.

Now with the tax incentive in place, a study by the United States Department of Agriculture (USDA) projects that the biodiesel demand will increase to at least 124 million US gallons per year.

In fact, if the price of crude oil skyrockets or environmental necessity, the industry estimates that the demand for biodiesel will be even higher in the upcoming decade.

Furthermore, the current production capacity that is made up of the hundreds of biodiesel plants and oleo-chemical companies that are already producing biodiesel is estimated to produces 150 million US gallons per year. It is believed that this number may double during the next 12-18 months, as there are currently various biodiesel production projects in the works.

In addition, since the tax incentive is predicted to create an economic surge, this means that the incentive could actually create as many as 50,000 jobs in the U.S. over the course of the next decade. It will also benefit farmers as it will increase the demand of soybean production, which will increase the price of soybean oil, but decrease the prices of soybean meal, resulting in the improvement of overall soybean value.

Hence it is expected that for every 100 million gallons of biodiesel, the cost of a bushel of soybeans will increase by US $0.10.

When all is said and done, with the help of the tax incentive, it is hoped that the prices of the biodiesel blend B20 will be lowered to match the cost as regular petroleum diesel fuel, which is roughly just over US $1.50 per gallon.

For more information about the biodiesel tax incentive visit the Biodiesel.org page
http://www.biodiesel.org/news/taxincentive/

In addition, if you would like a tax form and more information about your eligibility for fuel tax credit or refund, visit the IRS official government page at *http://irs.gov*

If in the United Kingdom:
http://www.hmrc.gov.uk/

Commercial Viability

There are many economic benefits for a nation when they make biodiesel commercially viable. As you have learned in Chapter 1, there are enough renewable resources in the U.S. and nearly everywhere else to make biodiesel commercially viable.

Not only that, but by choosing to make biodiesel commercially possible, the farmers of the U.S. gain financially from the production of biodiesel. This, in turn, also results in the financial gain of the economy, because the more consumers that use biodiesel, the less money will be spent on importing fuel.

The same goes for making biodiesel commercially viable in other nations of the world.

For instance, in India, it is becoming more and more imperative that the country increases its commercial viability.

This was discovered after a 2003-2004 economic survey revealed that petroleum products in India cost $20 billion U.S. dollars, which made up more than 30% of their total import bill. The survey also revealed that by increasing the use of B100 or B20, the crude oil import bill would drop by 20%.

Of course, aside from the economic financial benefit of making biodiesel commercially viable, countries benefit in other ways, as they improve upon the health of the environment and their people, by lowering emissions and preserving the quality of air.

To find out more about the benefits and disadvantages of biodiesel production, the next chapter covers everything you need to know.

Chapter 6
Benefits of Biodiesel

Did You Know...?

The benefits of biodiesel are vast. They assist us in every way that traditional fossil fuels do, plus in the ways that traditional diesel fuels are known to be disadvantageous, well they help in correcting that also.

The following are the primary benefits to biodiesel; however this list is by no means exhaustive (pun intended).

Environmental Benefits

This new millennium got off on an environmentally friendly note, when the year 2000 marked biodiesel as the first and only alternative fuel in the United States to have successfully completed the EPA (Environmental Protection Agency).

This is the governmental agency responsible for administration of laws to control and/or reduce pollution of air, water, and land systems-requirements in both Tiers I and II health effects testing within the EPA's Clean Air Act.

Lower Emissions

The tests were objectively performed by independent companies, and conclusively revealed the significant decrease in just about every regulated form of emissions, when using biodiesel. Furthermore, these tests demonstrated that biodiesel poses no known threat to human health.

Biodiesel and its emission contain neither sulphur nor aromatics.

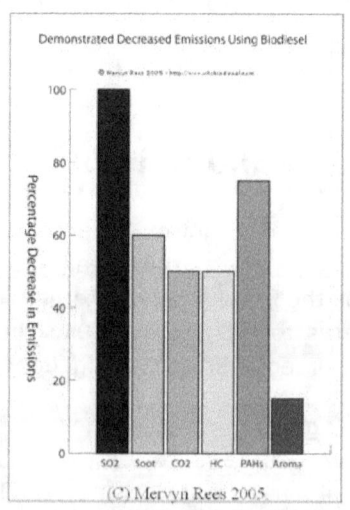

Figure 11
Graph Based on DOE USA Figures

The result of utilizing biodiesel within a standard diesel engine is a substantial decrease in the amount of unburned hydrocarbons, as well as carbon monoxide and particulate matter.

The Department of Energy in the United States demonstrated that both the production and the use of biodiesel – when compared to using traditional diesel fuel – allows for a 78.5% decreased in the emissions of carbon dioxide.

Biodiesel Emissions Compared to Regular Diesel

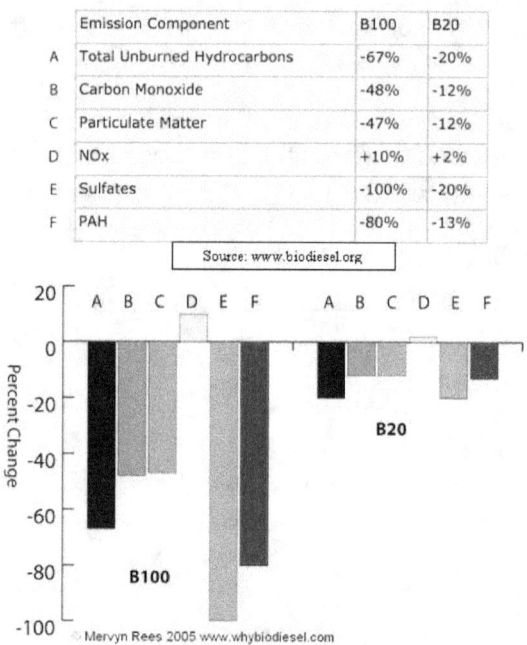

	Emission Component	B100	B20
A	Total Unburned Hydrocarbons	-67%	-20%
B	Carbon Monoxide	-48%	-12%
C	Particulate Matter	-47%	-12%
D	NOx	+10%	+2%
E	Sulfates	-100%	-20%
F	PAH	-80%	-13%

Source: www.biodiesel.org

Figure 12

Furthermore, biodiesel is recognized for its positive energy balance.

This means that for every unit of energy that is needed to create a gallon of biodiesel, there are 3.24 units of energy which are acquired.

Improvement of exhaust emissions when using biodiesel includes a substantial decrease in the following compounds:

1. Carbon monoxide

2. Hydrocarbons

3. Particulates

This being said, it should be noted that biodiesel exhaust includes approximately the same amount of nitrogen gas emissions as petroleum diesel fuels.

Consider the exponentially increasing demand for diesel – especially with the unpredicted world demand that has suddenly sprung up in the areas in and around China and India – then the inclusion of biodiesel as a partial replacement for petroleum-based diesel, or even a blending of the two, can make a substantial difference in the efforts to control greenhouse gasses.

Because of these lowered emissions, biodiesel becomes an ideal option for use in and around urban areas where air pollution has been difficult to control. Furthermore, such emission decreases make biodiesel a fuel more compatible within confined areas such as mines, in which ventilation and air circulation is a serious issue.

Decreased Toxicity

Biodiesel on its own – that is, when not mixed with traditional diesel – has an extremely low aquatic toxicity. Furthermore, it is entirely biodegradable within the span of approximately one month.

This feature of biodiesel is very environmentally important as it greatly decreases any impact of accidental biodiesel spills, making it much more practical for use in environmentally sensitive regions, such as inland waterways and other areas prone to devastation due to toxic spills.

Even when blended with petroleum-based diesel fuel, the toxicity level is vastly lowered, since its biodegradation experiences an acceleration of approximately three times the usual rate of traditional diesel.

Figure 13

Benefits in Energy Security

As petroleum prices reach highs that have been unheard of until today, and as agricultural prices simultaneously head towards record lows, it becomes obvious that if anything can be done to utilize domestic surpluses of vegetable oils in order to produce energy, it will be extremely favourable for bettering energy security.

Moreover, as it is quite possible to produce biodiesel by utilizing existing industrial production capacity, while using standard equipment, it means that there are a great deal of immediate opportunities available to attend to the current issues of energy security.

Should the actual cost of using foreign oil be compulsory for the cost of imported fuel, then renewable fuels – for example, biodiesel – would almost certainly be the most viable option.

For example, back in 1996, it was projected that the annual military costs for securing foreign oil would be $57 billion. Another approximately $4 billion annually went to foreign tax credits. Also, environmental costs ran at around $45 per barrel.

This means that for every billion dollars worth of foreign oil that was imported, there were 10,000 to 25,000 jobs that were lost – or that could not be created in the first place – within the United States alone.

Economic Benefits

The augmented use of renewable biofuels is an automatic lead towards notable micro-economic benefits within urban, suburban, and rural sectors alike, as well as with the balance of trade.

In 2001, the US Department of Agriculture completed a study, which discovered that should the average annual increase of the comparable soy-based biodiesel continue – that is, an increase of 200 million gallons per year – then the biodiesel demand alone would improve the total crop cash receipts by a staggering $5.2 billion by the year 2010.

This would produce an average net income increase for farms of approximately $300 million per year. Throughout that period, the factored increase in price per bushel of soybeans would be 17 cents per year.

Not only would this mean that biodiesel would allow us to support a domestically produced fuel that is a renewable alternative to diesel engines – both conventional and specific to biodiesel – but it would also allow us to benefit from its high performance characteristics. These include:

1. Increased cetane rating

2. High oxygen content

3. High fuel lubricity

All of these features result in a much cleaner, much better performing diesel product.

Benefits in Quality

Biodiesel is registered with the EPA both as a fuel in itself, as well as being registered as a fuel additive. In both cases, biodiesel meets the clean diesel standards, which have been set by the California Air Resources Board (CARB).

The formula B100 (that is, 100% biodiesel) has also received the designation as an alternative fuel by the United States Department of Energy, as well as the United States Department of Transportation.

Furthermore, the American Society of Testing and Materials (ASTM) approved the specification D6751 for biodiesel fuel in the year 2001. This was a vital benchmark in the standardization of biodiesel fuel quality in the American marketplace.

The trade association for the biodiesel industry, the National Biodiesel Board, created the National Biodiesel Accreditation Commission (NBAC) in order to audit procedures and marketers of the fuel, as well as to enforce the standards of biodiesel fuel quality within the United States.

In this effort, the NBAC issues seals of approval stating "Certified Biodiesel Marketer" to any biodiesel marketers who have met each of the requirements of the NBAC fuel accreditation audits.

This NBAC seal supplies customers and engine manufacturers with the additional confidence that they need by knowing that the seal's recipient meets the ASTM standards for biodiesel and that the marketer or producer in question will indeed back up its products and its claims.

Benefits with EPA Compliancy Requirements

Beginning in November of 1998, Congress approved biodiesel's use as being compliant with the Energy Policy Act (EPA)'s strategies. This decision permits fleets covered by the EPA (federal, state, and public utility) to utilize biodiesel in order to meet their alternative fuel vehicle purchase requirements.

To do so, they would need to purchase 450 gallons of B100 (100% biodiesel) and use it within either new or existing vehicles in a minimum of 20% blend with conventional petroleum-based diesel fuel.

Furthermore, the Congressional Budget Office as well as the U.S. Department of Agriculture, has established biodiesel as the alternative fuel that meets the Federal Government's EPA compliance requirements which results in the lowest overall cost.

The reason for this is simple: it works with existing, standard diesel engines. This way, the transition to the biodiesel alternative can be both immediate and seamless, and will instantly turn any diesel fleet into one that runs much more cleanly.

Performance Benefits

Many different countries including Canada, the United States, New Zealand, and most parts of Europe have been holding widespread testing of biodiesel within cars, trucks, trains, buses, farm equipment, and even small boats.

This testing effort has involved the use of B100 (100% biodiesel), as well as a range of different blends of biodiesel and petroleum based diesel.

The test findings have shown that the use of biodiesel reduces engine wear, while maintaining virtually the same performance level. Many of these tests have also demonstrated that the best overall results are achieved in vehicles with conventional diesel engines, when using a blend of 20% biodiesel with 80% petroleum-based diesel.

Benefits of Biodiesel vs. Other Alternative Efforts

Though biodiesel may be a much cleaner form of fuel than conventional petroleum-based diesel, it is estimated by some that this apparent advantage may diminish as emissions-reduction efforts continue to increase the efficiency of traditional combustion using petroleum-based diesel.

Additionally, biodiesel is currently facing fierce competition from other forms of alternative energy production that aim to reduce emissions while remaining cost-effective and maintaining performance. These alternatives include electricity, propane, and natural gas within some applications.

None of these, however, witness the secondary benefit seen by biodiesel production, in which it creates from three to six times more labour production per unit of production than fossil fuels currently provide. In today's employment market, that is an extremely attractive figure.

Drawbacks of Biodiesel

Although biodiesel does seem to be a miracle product, it is not without its faults. The importance is to balance its drawbacks with the larger picture to know whether or not you will be impacted in any way.

Some of the drawbacks of biodiesel have to do with the type of fuel that it is, and others have to do with its production and use on a much larger scale.

NO$_x$ Emissions

The primary issue to note with biodiesel itself is with its increased levels of NO$_x$ (Nitrogen Oxides, where the "X" is scientific notation for all the various combinations of possible Nitrogen Oxide) emissions. NO$_x$ is considered a serious air polluting emission, as it is very irritating.

This is not to say that biodiesel has greater NO$_x$ emissions than when using traditional petroleum-based diesel. However, NO$_x$ is the one air polluting emission that does not decrease by way of using biodiesel instead of conventional diesel. In fact, biodiesel exhaust contains approximately the same amount of nitrogen gas emissions as petroleum diesel fuels.

Frequently, in the production of diesel fuels, by decreasing the particulate matter quantities in the emissions, there is a consequent equivalent increase in the NO_x which are contributors to air pollution and "smog".

Some of these NO_x emission issues may be dealt with by making certain adjustments to the engine; however, this is not universally possible.

Some of the adjustment efforts and research studies to meet this need have included the following:

By adjusting the engine's injection timing and operating temperature, the NO_x emission levels in biodiesel exhaust can often be reduced to below the conventional petroleum-based diesel exhaust levels.

When using a properly adjusted engine, several researchers from the Department of Agricultural Engineering in the University of Idaho discovered that NO_x emissions could consistently be reduced to below traditional diesel exhaust levels. Dynamometer tests showed that with regular diesel fuel, the NO_x emissions started at 6.2gm per mile and decreased to about 5.6gm per mile with B100 (100% biodiesel), with a slightly larger decrease when using REE (rapeseed ethyl ester) instead of RME (rapeseed methyl ester).

When this information is factored in to the fact that B100 also reduce emissions levels from petroleum-based diesel in HC (hydrocarbons) by 53%, CO (carbon monoxide) by 50% and PM (particulate matter) by 13.5%, then the up to 10% possibility of reduction in NO_x remains very attractive from an emissions standpoint.

- By retarding fuel injection timing, NO_x emissions are consistently reduced, and other emissions maintain their standard biodiesel reductions.

- As the concentration of biodiesel – in a biodiesel/diesel fuel mixture – increased, so do the levels of NO_x in the emissions. Without any engine adjustments, the fuel blend B20A20 (20% biodiesel and 20% alkylate, with 60% low-sulphur petroleum diesel fuel) is currently the most effective means for reducing NO_x emissions below that of using only diesel fuel.

Additional engine adjustments, such as retarding the fuel injection timing and the operating temperature, biodiesel then becomes a very effective method of reducing NO_x emissions in a diesel engine.

1. Biodiesel emissions of NO_x increase or decrease depending on the testing procedures and the engine family being utilized. When testing for biodiesel NO_x emissions, the testing conditions, condition

of the diesel engine, ignition timing, and running temperature all play a role in the results. When the engine was changed and its running functions altered, test results ranged from NO_x emissions 10% lower than petrodiesel all the way to 13% higher than petrodiesel.

2. However, these tests also showed that since biodiesel lacks sulphur content, many NO_x controlling technologies can be developed and implemented which were not possible when using conventional diesel fuel.

3. Therefore, biodiesel's NO_x emissions are considered to be effectively and efficiently manageable, and it is expected that they will soon no longer be a concern when using the fuel.

4. When biodiesel suppliers Aiko Associates Ltd tested using the urban bus retrofit program with the EPA (Environmental Protection Agency), an oxidation catalyst was used to maximize the reductions in PM (particulate matter) – utilizing the biodiesel feature of its highly soluble organic fraction – and to make up for a slight increase in particulates when introducing a timing change which reduced

NO_x emissions to below regular diesel levels. In the best case, there was a 28% reduction in NO_x emissions, and a 25% reduction in PM emissions.

New technologies and alternatives are actively being researched on an international level in order to reduce the NO_x levels found in biodiesel emissions.

Behaviour as a Solvent

Another issue facing biodiesel use is that it can behave as a solvent. Though this is also a helpful property in its practicality, it can also be a disadvantage in some specific cases.

Some older diesel vehicles – not specific to any make or model, but usually in vehicles made before the year 1994 – might find that there is a clogging hazard when higher concentrations of biodiesel are utilized. The reason for this is that biodiesel, by nature, loosens deposits that have built up in the engine.

While this is quite beneficial for keeping the engine clean and running more efficiently, in older engines there may be quite a build-up from old traditional diesel fuel, causing the filter to become jammed with these freshly released deposits.

To combat clogging filters, it is recommended by most biodiesel manufacturers that when you use biodiesel, the fuel pump filters should be checked before first using biodiesel and then regularly cleaned /changed as necessary after switching to biodiesel.

This problem resolves itself as your whole fuel system rapidly cleans up.

Further issues are caused by the solvency of biodiesel, as it can contribute to the degradation of older fuel systems.

Additionally, biodiesel can act to break down the rubber components of older vehicles. Since some of the parts of older systems – for example fuel lines and fuel pump seals – are made of rubber, or rubber-like substances, these components can become broken down through high concentrations of biodiesel use.

To remedy this situation, it is recommended that such rubber and rubber-like components be replaced before, or shortly after, higher concentrations of biodiesel are used and why not add a line filter in an easily accessible place for ease of service especially in the early phase.

Though it is true that most manufacturers include biodiesel in their standard product warranties, there is still potential for issues to pop up.

Essentially the issue is that the vehicle manufacturer will warranty that their product (the vehicle) is free from material or manufacturing defects. Their warranty will also specify the fuels they expect the vehicle to use successfully.

On the other hand, fuel suppliers warranty their fuel, to be free of defects and to be the kind of fuel stated (octane ratings, lead free etc).

In the case of your biodiesel production, this means you are responsible for the fuel being free from defects or contaminants, and meeting the biodiesel standards.

Currently many manufacturers of diesel engine cars do specify suitable biodiesel for use with their engines.

The specification has two components; the standard of the biodiesel itself, commonly meaning that the biodiesel must meet the ASTM D-6751 standard. Second is the blend of biodiesel and petro-diesel. This is most commonly B20 or lower proportion of biodiesel.

For your personal use, it is important to check the warranty of the vehicles you intend to fuel. If you move into commercial production, you will of course need to warranty that your biodiesel meets the standard.

In the past most problems came from using biodiesel in older cars with rubber-type components which were liable to perish when in prolonged contact with biodiesel. Newer vehicles (post 1990 - however a few vehicles up to '94 still had rubber in their systems) are far less likely to have this problem.

If you find yourself with rubber in the tank connections or the fuel lines etc. simply replace with a synthetic product, readily available through normal suppliers.

Decrease in Fuel Economy and Power

Some engines may experience a small decrease in fuel economy and power when using biodiesel.

On average, in engines that experience this phenomenon, there is approximately 10% in power reduction.

Put into clearer terms, this means that for every 1.1 gallons of biodiesel, the engine will obtain the same amount of power as with 1 gallon of petroleum diesel but seldom noticed.

However by adjusting your engines 'timing' not only will you increase the power output from biodiesel but will also decrease engine noise and pollutants such as NO_x emission to way below that of regular diesel.

Cold Flow Properties

Another possible drawback that impacts both pure (B100) biodiesel and combinations of biodiesel and petrodiesel (such as the most highly used B20) is the cold flow properties.

Cold flow properties are the issues that occur when diesel – whether it be traditional diesel, biodiesel, or a combination of the two – is used when the mercury drops to very cold temperatures.

The United States Department of Agriculture has discovered that the cold filter "plugging" point of B20 (20% biodiesel) occurs at about 7° (F) higher than it does with petrodiesel.

Though this is a small increase in plugging temperature, for most B20 users, there have not been any noticeable problems.

However, should you have any problems in cold weather just increase the amount of regular diesel in your tank. Some manufacturers use an additive such as kerosene.

In fact, when the United States Department of Agriculture monitored Five Seasons Transportation's B20 use in Cedar Rapids, Iowa throughout one of the coldest recorded winters – where temperatures reached minus 20° F / = minus 29° C – no changes were made to the operation at all, and no noteworthy issues where aroused throughout their 1.4 million miles of operation.

Shelf Life

Another potential issue that has arisen with B100 and biodiesel mixes, such as B20, is its shelf life. Currently, the industry standard states that biodiesel – whether pure or in combinations – should be utilized within a six-month period as should fossil fuels.

This is not an issue, since most fuels are used well before six months, unless the operator happens to be storing fuel over extended periods of time. Already biodiesel manufactures are using Vitamin E as an Anti-Oxidant.

If storage is the case, it is recommended that fleet operators test their biodiesel fuel before it is used.

Retail Cost

Among the biodiesel drawbacks that occur on a broader scale are issues that are associated primarily with the market and connected logistics. Among these, the most significant is cost.

As per the observations of the EPA, B100 (100% biodiesel) can have a cost ranging e.g. from *$1.95 to *$3.00 per US gallon. Comparatively, B20 blends (20% biodiesel) usually cost an average of about $0.30 to $0.40 above the price of petrodiesel.

The actual cost is dependent upon many variables, chief of which is the type of plant crop or feedstock utilized, as well as the market conditions. With the cost of fossil fuels rising almost daily this will quickly reverse itself.

Quantities and Availability

Other than cost, the second most likely important issue concerning biodiesel is the quantities, which in the US alone grew to approximately 75 million gallons in 2005 accelerated to 250 million gallons in 2006 and as you can see in my graph, rapidly increasing through this last decade to an estimated 410 million gallons per annum by the end of 2009, with estimated projections for 2020 some 630 million gallons, that's a staggering 41,959 barrels a day.

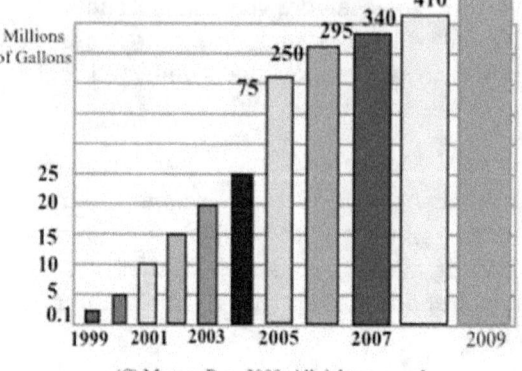

Figure 14

Biodiesel isn't necessarily produced in every country; however, it can be made anywhere. There are three primary ways in which you may procure biodiesel, (apart from the obvious one of making it yourself), each of which is geared towards different kinds of consumers.

1. Purchasing biodiesel directly from the manufacturer

2. Obtaining biodiesel from a petroleum distributor

3. Buying biodiesel at public pumps

There are a substantial number of National Biodiesel Board members, which currently produce /market biodiesel in the United States, but for the UK and other areas in the world check out *www.biodieselfillingstations.co.uk*

Interestingly enough, as biodiesel gains popularity, well-known figures are becoming involved, for example, Dow Chemical™ and World Energy™ (refer to Chapter 9 for more information), and – of all people – Willie Nelson.

To learn more about obtaining biodiesel, refer to Chapter 1, or visit one of the following websites:

National Biodiesel Board:
www.biodiesel.org/buyingbiodiesel/guide/

Alternative Fuels Data Centre:
www.eere.energy.gov/afdc/
(Search by state)

Additional information for locating biodiesel outside the United States can be obtained by contacting your local bio-fuel agency.

In the UK we have a super website called biodiesel filling stations the contact URL is: *www.biodieselfillingstations.co.uk*

On this site you will find terrific information and links to suppliers in UK, simply by clicking on their 'Biodiesel Outlets' button, and then click on the regional map where you are to locate a biodiesel supplier.

For those who live elsewhere in the world there is an 'Outlets Abroad' button which at the time I last looked had covered the countries of Australia. Austria, Germany, Holland, Ireland, Italy, Malta, Norway, Spain, Switzerland, and America and judging from reports are always looking for more, so check it out.

This site has very useful reading and great links to follow up on including a site I also know will be of interest namely 'Good Energy' found at *www.goodenergy.co.uk/*

Chapter 7
F.A.Q's (Frequently Asked Questions)

False or Truth? + Frequently Asked Questions!

As with any "new" forms of energy or technologies, many rumours, myths, and misunderstandings have popped up with regards to biodiesel. The following chapter segment will attempt to dispel some of the more popular rumours that have arisen regarding biodiesel, plus answering often asked questions.

1. What's the difference between regular diesel and biodiesel?

Regular diesel is a fuel made from mineral based oil (fossil fuel) whereas biodiesel is made from oils extracted from any oil seeds such soy bean, rapeseed, olives, peanuts palm, safflower, sunflower, castor etc, and other vegetable matter, and is often made from waste/used cooking oils and animal fats. Biodiesel is the cleanest burning diesel fuel, made from 100% natural, 100% renewable vegetable sources.

2. Why Biodiesel?

The major cause of pollution in the world is fossil fuel. Biodiesel offers a significant beneficial impact towards cleaning up our environment and using a renewable fuel. There is an immediate and dramatic reduction in particulate matter emissions and other targeted emissions. This helps to stabilize the dangerous greenhouse gases. In biodiesel we have a non-toxic, biodegradable and sulphur free sustainable fuel.

3. Is using biodiesel allowed in the USA, Europe etc.

Yes – You will find biodiesel in most parts of the world

4. What is B5, B20 or B100

Biodiesel is often labelled B20 for example, all this means is that that particular fuel is 20% biodiesel & 80% regular diesel, and relatively so for all the other 'B' numbers.

5. I have heard you need new filters when you change to biodiesel fuel.

When you start using biodiesel it is best to put in a new fuel filter and sometimes fit a new line filter in an accessible part of the fuel line because biodiesel will clean your fuel tank and fuel lines of the deposits left behind by the regular diesel and so at first you can get a blockage.

A cheap line filter is quick and easy to replace and after awhile you will find this problem soon disappears as the deposits left by fossil fuel (regular diesel) stop.

6. False – Biodiesel gives poor performance in cold weather.

Truth – While it is true that if the temperature gets cold enough, biodiesel will gel, it is also true that this is just as common in the customary regular petrodiesel.

Though B100 (pure biodiesel) does have a higher cloud point than petrodiesel, the more popular B20 blends are managed by using the exact same techniques as with pure conventional diesel. Biodiesel blends of anything lower than 5% have no impact whatsoever on the cold flow. It is also a fact that manufacturers use additives such as kerosene to offset cold weather problems, truckers used this technique for years in regular diesel for the same problem.

7. False – There is no impartial biodiesel fuel formulation standard in existence.

Truth – The biodiesel industry has been extremely vigorous in setting practical and accurate standards for biodiesel fuel and its blends since 1994 – the year that the first biodiesel task force was created in the ASTM (American Society for Testing and Materials). A biodiesel standard was provisionally approved by the ASTM in July of 1999 (it was called ASTM PS 121). In December of 2001, a final B100 (pure biodiesel) specification was issued (called D-6751).

8. False – The shelf life of biodiesel is too short to be practical.

Truth – No matter what kind of fuel you are using, it is always recommended that it be used up before six months have passed. This includes petroleum diesel also.

The fact is that most fuel – unless it is being stored – is used up long before six months passes.

The industry recommendation for biodiesel currently states that it should also be utilized within six months. Should it sit for a longer period than that, it should be re-tested before it is used, in order to make certain that it still meets the ASTM standards for D-6751.

The shelf life of biodiesel can be extended depending on its specific composition, and whether or not storage-enhancing additives have been used.

N.B. Never store biodiesel in concrete storage systems.

9. False – By using biodiesel, you may risk losing your engine manufacturers warranty.

Truth – Using biodiesel within existing diesel engines voids neither parts nor materials within workmanship warranties of any major engine manufacturer. Check manufacturer's handbook for explicit exceptions.

10. How does biodiesel help balance global warming?

The U.S. Department of Energy and the U.S. Department of Agriculture, concluded biodiesel reduces net CO_2 emission by 78 percent against using regular diesel. This is because biodiesel has a closed carbon cycle. This means CO_2 released into the atmosphere from biodiesel is recycled by growing plants, which are later processed into fuel completing the natural cycle.

11. What is the ratio of Methanol used?

Large biodiesel refineries use around a 35% methanol mix in their reactors, with this usage the easier the reaction will go. However the more methanol you use, the more you waste. In ideal conditions, reaction only uses around 10%. In reality, you will need 20% methanol to get a correct reaction. This is proved time and time again by home brewing aficionados.

12. What is the cost to making a gallon of biodiesel?

A lot of factors govern the cost of manufacturing, but for the small home brewers using recycled cooking oils, it generally comes out around $0.75 cents to a dollar per gallon, a non comparison cost of 45/60 pence a gallon in UK at the time of writing.

13. Do I have to pay fuel tax if I make my own biodiesel?

Small-scale blenders who produce less than 400 gallons per calendar quarter, have an exclusion from fuel excise taxes from the IRS. Rules will vary around the world; read my book where I discuss this more fully on page 85 and elsewhere.

14. False – biodiesel is an experimental alternative fuel and has not yet been thoroughly researched, tested, and assessed.

Truth – among all of the alternative fuels available today, biodiesel is one of the most thoroughly researched and tested.

Numerous independent studies have been performed, uniformly demonstrating that biodiesel has a very similar performance to conventional petroleum-based diesel, while it maintains important benefits to both the environment and to human health in comparison to its petrodiesel counterpart.

Such research has been performed by the United States Department of Energy and the United States Department of Agriculture, as well as the largest fuel injection equipment manufacturer in the United States, Stanadyne Automotive Corp.

Further studies have also been performed by the Lovelace Respiratory Research Institute and the Southwest Research Institute.

In fact, biodiesel is the first and the only form of alternative fuel to have completed and passed each of the Health Effects tests that are required by the Clean Air Act.

Biodiesel boasts performance levels very similar to conventional petroleum-based diesel in over 50 million successful miles on the road in effectively every kind of diesel engine, as well as in innumerable off-road and marine hours.

At this time, there are currently over 300 major fleets that utilize biodiesel.

15. False – Biodiesel does not achieve the same level of performance as petroleum-based diesel.

Truth – Among biodiesel's primary advantages is that it may be used in traditional diesel engines and fuel injection equipment without any notable impact to performance.

Biodiesel's cetane number is higher than that of petrodiesel fuel.

The cetane number is the measure of the ignition quality in diesel fuels.

The higher the cetane number of a fuel, the easier it is to ignite when it is injected into the diesel engine. Since biodiesel has a higher cetane number than conventional petroleum-based diesel, it means that it is easier to ignite in the engine's fuel injection system – meaning that it has the potential for better performance.

When B20 usage was observed in over 50 million miles of in-field demonstrations, it showed extremely similar results to petrodiesel in the areas of:

1. Fuel consumption

2. Horsepower

3. Torque

4. Haulage rates

Furthermore, biodiesel's lubricity is superior to petrodiesel, and has the highest BTU content of any alternative fuel, and ranging between the 1st and 2nd spot when compared to traditional diesel fuel.

The BTU (British Thermal Units) content is the energy of a fuel, measured per gallon. The higher the BTU content, the more power can be drawn from each gallon of the fuel to be consumed.

Since biodiesel has a higher BTU content than any other alternative fuel, and is so closely comparable to the BTU content of conventional diesel, it means that biodiesel has higher energy content per gallon than any other alternative fuel, and close matches that of petrodiesel.

16. False – Using biodiesel will plug filters.

Truth – biodiesel – blended with petrodiesel – can be utilized within any kind of diesel engine, with or without any modifications to the engine or its fuel system.

When using B100, however, it can have a solvent effect on engines that have not been calibrated and altered specifically for biodiesel use. This biodiesel solvency may cause deposits that have accumulated within the tank and the pipes from previous petrodiesel use to be released. These freed deposits may then clog filters when the biodiesel is first being used.

This problem can be prevented simply by replacing fuel filters until the system has cleaned itself and build-up release finishes and no longer occurs.

When using B20 blends, plugging of filters is unlikely and uncommon, even so, normal serving filter checks sort variations.

17. False – Lower blends of biodiesel in petrodiesel are prohibitively expensive.

Truth – The picture changes daily as the price per barrel of fossil fuel increases, and more and more biodiesel is being made. Company made fuels bear costs that homemakers do not such as:

The Fuel • The Transportation • The Storage • The Blending

Any increase in cost comes alongside a noticeable increase in diesel quality, as lower blends of biodiesel dramatically improve the lubricity etc of the diesel fuel.

Another plus being the fluid price situation and cost are relative, so as fossil fuel prices continue to rise, it makes biodiesel even more of a bargain.

18. False – Biodiesel degrades engine seals and gaskets.

Truth – Recently, with the switch to diesel of lower sulphur levels, most OEMs (Original

Equipment Manufacturers) have switched to engine components that are suitable for use with biodiesel.

Overall, B100 did soften or degrade some kinds of natural rubber and elastomers over a period of time in older vehicles, some up to 1994.

This is easily rectified by using modern materials to replace them.

By using blends of a higher percentage, fuel system components can be affected – mainly in fuel hoses and fuel pump seals – when they include elastomers compounds that are not compatible with biodiesel.

This impact is decreased as the amount of biodiesel in the blend is lessened.

For example, in the B20 formula, no changes to hoses and gaskets are required.

19. False – There is no impartial biodiesel fuel formulation standard in existence.

Truth – The biodiesel industry has been extremely vigorous in setting practical and accurate standards for biodiesel fuel and its blends since 1994 – the year that the first biodiesel task force was created in the ASTM (American Society for Testing and Materials).

A biodiesel standard was provisionally approved by the ASTM in July of 1999 (it was called ASTM PS 121).

In December of 2001, a final B100 (pure biodiesel) specification was issued (called D-6751).

Biodiesel is defined as the mono alkyl esters of long chain fatty acids derived from vegetable oils or animal fats, for use in compression-ignition (diesel) engines. This specification is for pure (100%) biodiesel prior to use or blending with diesel fuel.#

Property	ASTM Method	Limits	Units
Flash Point	D93	130 min.	Degrees C
Water & Sediment	D2709	0.050 max.	% vol.
Kinematic Viscosity, 40 C	D445	1.9 - 6.0	mm^2/sec.
Sulfated Ash	D874	0.020 max.	% mass
Sulfur	D5453		
S 15 Grade		15 max.	ppm
S 500 Grade		500 max.	
Copper Strip Corrosion	D130	No. 3 max.	
Cetane	D613	47 min.	
Cloud Point	D2500	Report	Degrees C
Carbon Residue 100% sample	D4530**	0.050 max.	% mass
Acid Number	D664	0.80 max.	mg KOH/gm
Free Glycerin	D6584	0.020 max.	% mass
Total Glycerin	D6584	0.240 max.	% mass
Phosphorus Content	D 4951	0.001 max.	% mass
Distillation Temp. Atmospheric Equivalent Temperature, 90% Recovered	D 1160	360 max.	Degrees C

Figure 15

To meet special operating conditions, modifications of individual limiting requirements may be agreed between purchaser, seller and manufacturer.

The carbon residue shall be run on the 100% sample.

A considerable amount of experience exists in the US with a 20% blend of biodiesel with 80% diesel fuel (B20). Although biodiesel (B100) can be used, blends of over 20% biodiesel with diesel fuel should be evaluated on a case-by-case basis until further experience is available.

Information of biodiesel specifications is available from the ASTM website at *www.astm.org.*

20. False – The United States does not yet have the infrastructure in place for the prevention of biodiesel shortages.

Truth – Today, there are over 14 companies who have invested millions of dollars for developing biodiesel production plants that actively market the product.

By examining current biodiesel manufacturing abilities and the long-term processing agreements, there is a present capacity of over 200 million gallons of biodiesel.

There are many facilities, which are able to double their biodiesel production capacity within an eighteen-month period.

For more information about biodiesel plants, refer to Chapter 9.

21. False – The biodiesel industry's development is not supported by single government program.

Truth – As of January of 2001, the United States Department of Agriculture announced its implementation of the first program to supply price incentives for manufacturing 36 million gallons of biodiesel.

The use of biodiesel and ethanol is also supported by bills that were introduced to the United States Congress in 2003.

This includes a bill that sets the renewable standard for American fuels, as well as one, which provides biodiesel with a partial fuel excise tax exemption.

Over a quarter of American states have passed positive biodiesel legislation with, I am told, more on the way.

Chapter 8
Algae

The Miracle Which Is Algae

As many methods as there are already for making biodiesel – as discussed to great extent in Chapter 3 – there is always room to find new methods of production. After all, the more ways there are to make it, the more practical it becomes.

One of the leading techniques being studied for future biodiesel manufacturing is through the use of algae ponds and waste lagoons

Among the primary benefits of using algae crops is the fact that it is extremely easy to grow. However, it is also important to consider that for algae, you can grow 3 crops in one month, as opposed to 1 crop in an entire season as is the case for oil seed crops.

For example, one serious consideration would be to use the waste lagoons from water treatment plants to grow several algae crops every month, and produce exactly what is needed for cheap, high-performance biodiesel.

In fact, the prospects are so good that algae are being called "the crop of the future" by many, including members of the chemical engineering department of Mississippi State University.

Since waste lagoons and good algae climate are extremely easy to come by, algae growth for potential oil crops is twice as easy and practical, producing twice as much oil as soy crops, while still making high-dollar, healthy, long-lived products.

Approximately 50% of the weight of diatom algae (any of various microscopic one-celled or colonial algae of the class Bacillariophyceae, having cell walls of silica consisting of two interlocking symmetrical valves) is oil.

There are many potential areas for algae cultivation. These include:

1. Animal waste lagoons

2. Waste streams

3. Food-producing fish ponds (which would be symbiotic production).

4. Oceans

The United States Department of Energy has estimated that by utilizing algae crops, we could achieve over 15,000 gallons per acre, per year.

When compared to the average canola yield of 300 gallons per acre, per year, this is a substantial improvement.

In fact, the Department of Energy believes that algae cultivation's potential is to not only replace petrodiesel entirely within the United States, but across the globe. Using unproductive land, in out of the way regions such as deserts, (so called Badlands) algae can thrive with saline water; use human and animal refuse to feed on, and much more.

The Chemical Miracle of Algae

Among the key reasons that algae are such an ideal solution for biodiesel production is that it is photosynthetic.

Photosynthesis is the process, which allows plants, algae, and some types of bacteria to transform energy from the sun into energy that can be used by all forms of organic life on earth.

The photosynthetic process involves the combination of water (H2O) with carbon dioxide (CO_2) in order to create biomass; also called living matters.

Once it was determined by biofuels programs that terrestrial plants can be sources of fuel, the next logical step was to look into photosynthetic organisms growing within aquatic environments.

Such aquatic photosynthetic organisms include:

1. Macro algae (best known as seaweed)

2. Micro algae (unicellular photosynthetic aquatic plants)

3. Emergent (rooted aquatic plants which extend above the water)

Macro algae, or seaweed, are an extremely fast growing form of both marine and freshwater plants, some of which are able to attain substantial sizes of up to 60 meters in length.

Emergents are plants which grow partially submerged, but which extend onto or above the water of bogs and marshes, such as cattails and water lilies.

Micro algae, on the other hand, are photosynthetic organisms on a microscopic level. Just like macro algae, micro algae are located in both marine environments as well as in freshwater.

Though research began with all three types of aquatic photosynthetic organisms, focus quickly changed exclusively to micro algae as its true potentials began being discovered throughout the research.

This potential includes the fact that micro algae simply produce a great deal more of the natural oils that are compatible for bio-fuels such as biodiesel.

This was not known initially, as the study of micro algae has been relatively limited until this point. Until its discovery for biodiesel uses, algae had not been nearly as well understood as other organisms that have become a part of the biodiesel industry.

Of course, as with other forms of organisms, there are many types of algae. Biologists have divided them into a number of classes, primarily determined by pigmentation, life cycle, and their cellular makeup. In terms of availability, the four most important forms of algae are:

1. Diatoms (Bacillariophyceae) – these are the algae, which make up the majority of oceanic phytoplankton. They are also found in both fresh and brackish waters. There are approximately one hundred thousand different species of diatom algae known to us today.

2. Diatom algae contain polymerized silica (Si) in their cellular walls. Since all living cells store carbon in different forms, diatoms store them in the form of natural oils or as the carbohydrate polymers called chyrsolaminarin.

3. Green algae (Chlorophyceae) – also plentiful, especially in freshwater, green algae can occur either as single cells or in colonies (such as one would discover in a swimming pool that needs maintenance).

4. Green algae are considered to be the evolutionary ancestors of today's modern plants. Their main storage compound is starch, though under certain circumstances they are known to produce oils.

5. Blue-green algae (Cyanophyceae) – this is the form of algae most similar in structure to bacteria. Blue-green algae are an important part of the nitrogen fixing cycle in the earth's atmosphere.

6. Currently, there are approximately 2,000 known blue-green algae species in a range of different habitats.

7. Golden algae (Chrysophyceae) – similar to diatoms in pigmentation and biochemical composition, golden algae have much more complex pigmentation systems, appearing, orange, yellow, or brown.

There are approximately 1,000 known species of golden algae, and they are found primarily in freshwater systems.

Golden algae's storage compounds consist both of natural oil and carbohydrates.

When algae were first being studied as a source of biodiesel, only two classes of algae were being collected: diatoms and green algae.

The photosynthetic mechanism within algae is comparable to that of plants higher along the evolutionary chain; however, they are much more efficient solar energy converters as a result of their cellular simplicity.

Furthermore, since micro-algal cells are always in aquatic suspension, their access to water (H_2O), carbon dioxide (CO_2) and other nutrient is much more efficient. Therefore, micro algae are able to create fifty times more oil per area of land, in comparison to terrestrial oilseed crops.

What does this mean in terms of biodiesel?

It means that algae are an ideal and efficient form of biological producer of high-density liquid energy in the form of natural oil, by utilizing a substance (CO_2) otherwise considered to be waste (zero-energy).

New Zealand - Wairau Sea Logoons
Biodiesel from Algae Research Area
© Mervyn Rees 2007

Concepts in Algae Production

This section will discuss the basics of how algae can be utilized in order to produce biodiesel. I will not go into too much depth for the manufacture of the biodiesel itself, as that is thoroughly covered in Chapter 3. Instead, it will discuss the process in which the algae are involved.

In order to harvest the oil produced by algae, it must be available in repeated crops of some quantity.

This can be achieved in waste pools, lagoons, water treatment plants, and animal waste pools. The area in which the algae are grown is called an algae farm.

The farm must be set up in a way that the algae will grown in a shallow, open pond in which ample CO_2 is available to be captured by the algae, as per the process in the diagram:

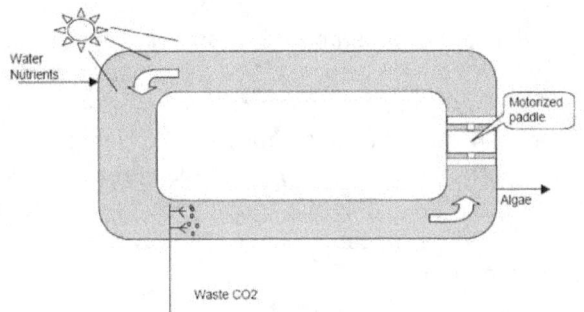

Figure 16
A Look Back at the U.S. Department of Energy's Aquatic Species Program Biodiesel from Algae

These algae farms are the "raceway" design, where algae, water, and necessary nutrient (for example, the source of the CO_2) are circulated around a racetrack shaped pond.

To continue the flow, paddlewheels are set in motion. Using this method, the algae remains consistently suspended within the water, while regularly being circulated to the surface of the water.

There are many different sources available for CO_2, where the algae farm would simply be using waste CO_2. These sources include any operation which combusts fuel in order to produce energy. So far, research has focused primarily on coal and other fossil fuel powered plants as the primary CO_2 source.

Consider that the standard coal plant emits flue gas which contains up to 13% CO_2. Such a high degree of CO_2 permits great ease of relocation and absorption into the algae farms. By pairing coal plants with algae farms, we are enabled to recycle the plant's CO_2 – a contributor to the green house effect – as a useable liquid fuel without such harmful emissions.

Another larger producer of CO_2 is from animal waste, such as cattle, sheep, and pig manure. Even chicken waste, when gathered properly, has a high nutrient value for crops, with its 40% protein content.

This is already beginning to make manure a competitive industrial commodity, in order to obtain it for the biogas it will produce. It is also valuable since it is so easy to obtain, it is economically viable, and does not cause additional environmental harm.

Just think of all the sewage from us humans, no matter how poor a country, this potential gigantic resource, a huge free supply of energy.

Well algae sure helps with a growing problem – it has always been said where there is muck there's money, - and Yes it is happening, fuel is already being made from it!

Algae farms must always be shallow to ensure the maximum amount of exposure in order to ensure the highest level of energy production and storage (as oil).

If the farm is too deep, the sunlight will be unable to penetrate deep enough to reach the lower levels of algae.

The algae farms will be under constant operation. This means that there will constantly be water and "nutrients" fed into the pond, and algae-filled water will be removed at the other end of the "racetrack". At that end, a harvesting system is required to recover the oil containing algae.

The size of the algae farm is determined by its surface area, not its volume.

Algae farm productivity is measured by way of daily biomass production per unit of the farm's surface area. For this reason, it is important to have a rather large area for the farm, so that multiple "racetracks" will be possible.

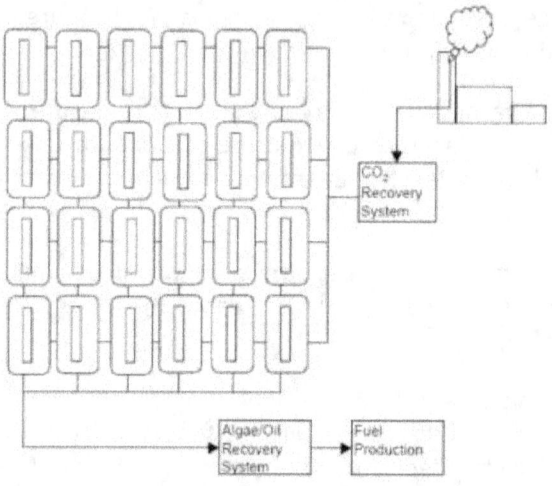

Figure 17

Naturally, the racetrack design is not the only available algae farm design. However, it is the most highly studied within the United States at the present.

Other governments, though, such as those of Japan, France, and Germany, are investing in considerable research for algae producing closed bioreactor reactors.

The reason for the preference of a closed algae farm as opposed to the open format of the racetrack is that they run less of a risk of contamination with other organisms and spores that may be carried in by the air.

Furthermore, as per the Japanese optical fibre-based reactor system design, a great deal less surface area is required for algae production in a closed style.

The downside of these latest systems of study is their prohibitive costs compared to their fuel production.

This is what primarily accounts for the American Department of energy's choice to focus instead on the open raceway systems, which have a much lower cost.

Chapter 9
The Future of Biodiesel Production

Engines and the Future

Biodiesel is an alternative fuel that is very safe for replacing conventional petroleum diesel.

This is due to its high lubricity, and its cleanliness in burning, as well as the fact that it can also be easily utilized as a diesel supplement in unmodified conventional diesel engines.

This being said, what does the future look when it comes to diesel engines and the introduction of biodiesel?

This is a question that is being heavily studied, especially with the building threat of Peak Oil, the worldwide oil issue caused by Hurricane Katrina in August of 2005, and the augmenting air pollution crisis.

Fossil Fuels and Peak Oil

Aside from the major issue that fossil fuels are major environmental pollutants which have, and continue to damage the earth and its oceans and atmosphere beyond repair. It has been discovered, beyond a doubt, that fossil fuels do have a limit as to their availability.

The focus now has moved towards a problem called "Peak Oil".

This refers to the time when oil extraction has reached its highest limit and begins its decline. Though it is impossible to determine when precisely Peak Oil will occur, what is known is that it will happen, and that we won't know it until we've reached it.

Some experts believe that we are reaching Peak Oil right now, while others claim that it is not yet reached, but it is not long off.

World Oil Finds and Production

Figure 18
2005 Interpretation of Oil Finds & Production

What does this mean? It means that gas and oil prices will continue to rise, and at a faster rate. It also means that many important decisions will need to be made regarding the way that the oil we do have can be used. Oil is used in an extremely large number of products.

The increasing problem of Peak Oil revolves around two other serious factors: the growing population of the world, and the increasing need for oil in developing countries.

As the population grows around the world, so will the demand for fuels, energies, food, and plastics; these are all products that depend very heavily on oil.

It is predicted that by the year 2050, the population of the world will grow from 6.5 billion by 2.6 billion, reaching 9.1 billion; all of which will need to be provided with food, supplies, and energy.

Further to the growth of the population, the augmented need for oil in developing nations – which have until today been consuming very little in petro-products – is putting a great deal of unpredicted strain on the oil market.

Production Agreement with Dow and World Energy

World Energy and Dow Haltermann Custom Processing (part of Dow Chemical) are setting an example for optimism in the renewable fuel industry, signing production agreements together, allowing Dow to supply World Energy with biodiesel. The goal is to enhance World Energy's current and future biodiesel production and distribution abilities.

This partnership between the entrepreneurial bio-energy firm, 'World Energy' and the world's leading chemical producer, Dow Chemical, has achieved great things in the advancement of biodiesel. Dow Haltermann Custom Processing (DHCP) will be producing biodiesel in Houston solely for 'World Energy' in North America.

Both companies agree that the partnership of DHCP's global reputation for excellence in chemical manufacturing, and World Energy's meticulous consideration for quality biodiesel production, creates a winning combination not only for the companies, but for the environment, the consumer, and the opinion and recognition of biodiesel as a viable alternative fuel.

Already, many private and public organizations are utilizing this company's biodiesel, including every Branch of the US Military

The most popular blend is the B20 (20% biodiesel and 80% petrodiesel), due to its ability to reduce emissions and be used within conventional diesel engines without alteration. Refer to Chapter 5 for further information about the advantages of B20.

This new production partnership is considered to be an important step towards helping America – and encouraging the world – to decrease its excessive dependency on oil – particularly foreign oil.

Biodiesel Plants

As was shown in Chapter 3, biodiesel is essentially made when vegetable oil or animal fat has a chemical reaction with an alcohol. This results in an alkyl monoester compound, which can work as a diesel fuel, but with much better emissions than petroleum diesel.

Within the United States, there are an extremely large number of biodiesel plants already in operation, and maps and tables demonstrate just a moment in time check link:
www.biodiesel.org/buyingbiodiesel/producers_mar keters/ProducersMap/existingandpotential.pdf

NB: Active plants are those companies that are producing biodiesel.

The United States is among the leading nations with current and planned biodiesel plants, but around the world there are already a large number of biodiesel plants and countries are working hard to add to their current numbers, for example:

- Canada

- Australia

- Most of the European Union

- Japan

- Argentina

- China

- India

- Malaysia

- And many more.

Two of the largest biodiesel plants are located in Australia (Natural Fuel Darwin Ltd) and the United States (Cargill Inc), owned by Lurgi-developed Multipurpose Technology, producing many hundreds of tonnes of biodiesel every day from palm and soybean oils.

A similar plant in Spain (Técnicas Reunidas) was designed to produce 144 tonnes per day using rape seed, soybean and palm oils.

Organizations around the world are helping with this process by allowing businesses to become involved in the biodiesel process.

This includes investing in a local plant, and taking part in its manufacture, such as allowing local farms to take part in the biodiesel industry through the waste that their farms already produce, but can now be utilized to make biodiesel.

In the United States, organizations such as Ascendant Partners (website at *www.AscendantPartners.com*) which is founded by three former CoBank staff members who have a great deal of experience in financing start-up biodiesel plants.

Therefore, they provide expert consulting services to food, agribusiness, and renewable energy organizations in order to help them to achieve their maximum potential.

Such businesses are having a great impact on encouraging the biodiesel boom which is well on its way.

Chapter 10

Why Choose a Biodiesel Compatible Car

If you are an average driver, you might find that biodiesel is a much better alternative than diesel or gasoline for you. There are a great number of ways by which you can benefit from using biodiesel on a regular basis.

Beyond the fact that oil prices are unstable, biodiesel is an extremely cost effective alternative, you'll also be able to enjoy the other advantages laid out in the "Benefits of Biodiesel" section of Chapter 6.

In the face of change

Let's face it we have all been changing to diesel engines for four reasons:

1. More Miles per Gallon.

2. Cheaper Fuel.

3. Cheaper to service.

4. Alternative fuel supplies.

So what happened?

- Diesel Engine cars cost more.

- Diesel prices go up.

- We are paying more taxes.

So by making your own biodiesel, you avoid all this as you discover the biodiesel secrets contained within this 'The Book on Biodiesel' your cost effective answer.

Biodiesel Compatible Cars - etc

100% biodiesel made to International standards such as EN14214 or ASTM 6751 will work just fine in any diesel engine, and in any ratio with or without fossil fuels, and you can switch back and forth as many times as you like, so rest easy.

With very modern high tech and up to date diesel vehicles and systems, from super racers to jet planes, you are working with and carry out maintenance and settings to the highest standards, and using high grade, dry-washed and polished biodiesel – Yes – even you too are fine.

The Yellowstone Park vehicle pictured below has run on100% biodiesel from new, and at time of writing had already covered 195,000 miles. I believe it is now in the park's museum in first class order, and another new vehicle has taken on its magnificent mantel!

Source: Yellowstone Park

So as I have said before:

Go on – Have a Ball – Knock your Socks Off!

Coming Soon

Diesel Motorcycles

Diesel engine motorcycles are not new as such. However to update you – information on diesel motorbikes, well I have been looking on the web and find surprising developments in this field.

Britain's Royal Military College of Science and California firm Hayes Diversified Technologies, using a stock Kawasaki KLR650 are jointly developing the first purpose built diesel motorcycle engine, designed especially for military use.

So in May 2001, a motor cycle known as the M1030M1 was born and in 2009 is only available for military use.

British, US and NATO forces, are looking to use this 580cc diesel motorcycle, for a more efficient military machine with less fuel consumption than petrol equivalents, better cross-country ability, lower emissions and 125 mpg, with top speed of around 85 mph.

The object is to design and develop a diesel motorcycle to meet the requirement for NATO armed forces, to run entirely on diesel fuel or aviation kerosene, for their entire inventory, getting rid of the need for petroleum and associated fire risks, also dramatically helping their logistics at the same time.

This new single cylinder diesel engine is being designed for many uses in other plant and equipment such as lightweight all-terrain vehicles [ATVs] or tractors, compressors, generators and the like as I understand it, with all the advantages that will bring.

Plus it would be on the cards to develop this purpose built diesel engine into a twin cylinder engine for light aircraft.

Source: University Press
www.cranfield.ac.uk

The Dutch Diesel Motorcycle

There is the sparkling 1200cc, Thunder Star 1200 TDI Sports bike, made by a Dutch company, StarTwin have used the VW Lupo, 3 cylinder diesel engine as the base unit.

Having worked their special kind of magic on it, Direct Injection, Turbo, Intercooler etc, added a suitable new gearbox, and designed and built their own frame. The end result is something very special indeed, a bike of outstanding performance and very low running costs.

Check it out on
www.gizmag.com/go/4273/picture/12824/

This website carries a host of photos of the 'Thunder Star' for the enthusiasts amongst you plus the various articles to discuss further.

A New Engine Design another diesel nugget for you – check it out at *www.scuderigroup.com*

Well I just thought I would show how diesel is developing. It's no wonder when you think of costs of fossil fuels, the extra mpg you get from diesel, and now biodiesel with its very low emissions, and you can make it for yourself, so can the military, they could do the same in the field – just stop and think – and the more you think about biodiesel the better it becomes.

So you can ponder the evolution of transport from one wheel to multi-wheeled over the last 100 years or so, I will just pop in some 'Pics' to get you all A-go-in' !

1928 Humber MC 350cc Side Valve

They say my side-valve Humber is the only one known left in existence?

As I do not ride anymore I have to find a new owner for her, so reluctantly she now is available to the right person.

Chapter 11
The Last Piece of the Puzzle

So here we are; I have brought you my reader through the magic of the written word to this point in our journey together into the world of biodiesel, where your thoughts on the making of your own supply of fuel whether it is for your vehicle, power or heating or all three of them have practically crystallized.

Now its decision time; how are you actually going to manufacture the biodiesel you need for your personal requirements?

You now have the knowledge, and know 'The Book on Biodiesel' as I promised, and now is the time for me to give you the last piece of the jigsaw!

Enjoy!

Making or Buying Your Own

Biodiesel Processors/Reactor

Biodiesel processors or reactors as some folk call them, conjure up all sorts of myths, worries, facts and rumours.

A world where some get excited at the thought of building their very own biodiesel producing machine, a machine to beat all known others machines.

Some look with trepidation and a fear of the black arts, and the stories they have heard of things going bump in the night etc.

Practically everyone searches the internet for clues. Can they find plans for building, lists of parts, scrap-heap foraging, expeditions to junk yards for the elusive trophy, or collar hold the local plumber to scrounge an old water heater?

Yep there are a lot of 'Apple Seed' reactors out there, and darned clever they are, some right genius, and good on 'em!

To each their own and yep it's good fun and very rewarding so why not?

Well hobby wise – I say, as long as you know what you are about, go for it, have fun, but please make sure you and yours are safe.

For the family who want day in, day out, quality biodiesel for their everyday use, whether in their car, truck, generator or heating system, and intend to be more than just a hobby then this is where it gets down to serious considerations.

Those that are thinking further ahead will need to consider how much biodiesel they will want to produce, and still leave some reserve built in for expansion.

Some will be thinking bigger still, they may have their own fleet of trucks, buses or taxi's.

Others will think about supplying it to neighbours, or starting Co-operatives.

Ideas are endless – yep there is a great big world out there, so think positively, think internationally, look at what is out there, carefully check out what you actually get for your hard earnt bucks, check potential life span of equipment, the built in safety standards, the materials used and ask why they use them.

Standards are being gradually imposed around the world on types of materials used in manufacture, highest standard electrical switches, and run-dry flameproof pumps, top quality safe heating elements built in thermometers etc.

First you have to make sure you have safety with long term reliability in your chosen equipment.

So check for notices and markings such as

CE – European standards, or UL – US Standards etc from country of origin which are acceptable internationally.

Next you must check out the claims made by suppliers,

e.g. this machine will produce say, 15,000 litres per day and cost so much less than other manufacturers equipment! Well that's what they say. What they fail to tell you is that theirs may well require extra equipment to achieve this claim; hence the actual cost may turn out to be a more expensive option after all.

We have to take note of where and why various manufacturers use differing materials.

Also – where they position an assembly, this way or that way, and why, where they place the pump, what to automate, and why, what not to automate, and why.

The ventilation must be adequate in all circumstances, the process controlled at all times day and night, so be aware of paying peanuts and getting a monkey!

High quality, safe and long lasting equipment, may not appear at first to be the best value for your hard earned money.

That's when the thinking person realizes that, with the money saved by making their own fuel, and the fact that a good processor will run and run long after other equipment needs repairing or replacing, it would simply be a false economy not to buy wisely.

What's more, with the ever-changing safety standards, you have to be aware that governments can outlaw cheaper alternatives, so having to replace poorer equipment sooner than planned.

I am not saying you have to go out and find the most expensive processor you can, but on the other hand you don't want your garden shed burning down in the middle of the night.

No on the contrary, I have know of some very expensive machines that do not meet the highest standards either in materials used, quality of electrical equipment and/or design.

So the task I set myself was to find Biodiesel Processors/Reactors with the following 'Wish' list:

1. Highest Standards of Manufacture

2. Giving Highest International Safety Standards

3. Highest Quality Materials & Equipment – ATEX approved.

4. Quality Construction

5. Compact Safe & Efficient Design

6. Built in Wash System

7. Custom Design Methoxide System

8. Fit for Purpose, capable of producing to highest standards consistently

9. Ease of Use day in day out

10. Long Lasting

11. Excellent Manufactures Guarantee and after-sales Service back-up

12. Overall Best Value for My/Your Money.

Also when talking about a really high output of top quality biodiesel, in a minimum time frame, you can manufacture processors with a built in industrial separator (centrifuge) for biodiesel, made as an exceptional high quality stainless steel separator with explosion proof motor (ATEX), which will separate the glycerine from the biodiesel in a much shorter time from than the normal necessary 8 hours.

Talking of stainless steel, this is a wonderful, if expensive material; some manufacturers are producing their reactors/processors in stainless steel.

This expensive option is claimed by some to solve all potential reactor material problems. Well in a perfect world this might be true. However because of some manufacturing techniques used, this is not always so.

As they say, "sauce for the goose, is sauce for the gander". In other words every material has its own set of potential problems if used incorrectly, so of course stainless steel has its issues also.

For example crevice corrosion and pitting or sometimes, where welding has taken place, there can be a high possibility of cracking caused through material stresses and corrosion. In fact a ventilation fault and/or heating element problems could, in fact, in certain adverse situations, cause a catastrophic explosion which would be greatly enlarged through the use of all metal construction.

So make sure that fail safe, pre-explosion-detecting sensing equipment is fitted.

Stainless steel lacks the 'at a glance' visual confirmation of fluid levels. You can have a viewing tube running up the outside of the processor to give a fluid indication level. This works OK as long as it's independent of the circulation tap being open.

So to each their own, it mostly depends on a suitable material to be chosen for the job in hand at the time, and working with it correctly to the highest standards.

When products that are built to comply with all required CE/UL standards they should always be accompanied with an official 'CE/UL Declaration of Conformity Certificate'. Individual parts like pumps or heating elements etc will also be stamped to clearly show this.

Consideration should also be given to the portability of your equipment. If this is important to you, then one would naturally think of its weight and one of the reasons why differing manufacturers choose how to build their various machines as this will also affect your choice.

You can see there are many factors beside the 'price' to take into account when calculating which processor/ reactor you buy.

It boils down to your own specific needs and requirements to find that 'fit for purpose processor/reactor', and having assessed these, you look for the following:

1. Check for safety standards. – ATEX directed

2. Quality of construction and the individual parts – CE/UL stamped

3. Value for money. – What you actually receive for your money, and whether you will need any extra equipment to produce the number litres/gallons of biodiesel required daily.

4. Be aware of differing measurement value around the world before you make your choice.

What I mean is 12,000 litres – 3,170 Gallons or is it 2,640 Gallons?

Well the point is, are they US gallons or Imperial (UK) gallons.

Well how can I check the numbers? I hear you say –

Well check out the following:

Litres into US gallons - divide by 3.7855

i.e. 12,000 litres ÷ 3.7855 = 3,170 US gallons.

US Gallons into Litres is Number of gallons multiplied by 3.7855

i.e. 3,170 US Galls. X 3.7855 = 12,000 litres.

Litres into imperial Gallons - divide by 4.546

i.e. 12,000 litres ÷ 4.546 = 2,640 Imperial gallons.

Imperial Gallons to Litres is Number of gallons multiplied by 4.546

i.e. 2,640 Imp galls. X 4.546 = 12,000 litres.

So there you have it. If anyone claims that their machine manufactures whatever number of gallons at a time, and does not state which 'type' of 'gallons', well now you can use these tools to make sure you know what you are buying, and get best value for your money.

5. Make sure to carefully check manufacturer's guarantees and after-sales care/service.

So which machine do I recommend?

Well because of my afore mentioned words on the subject, it will quickly rule in, or indeed rule out equipment, without my mentioning names, in this ever changing world of innovation and experience.

Enough to say when customers vote with their feet and pocket book/wallet, standards will rapidly rise and prices will become economic, it is the rule of the market, we all have the power to influence, no matter how small our part may be.

"Come on Merv, get off the fence", I hear you say, **"which one do you use?"**

Well there are a lot of great processors out there, so I had to focus my personal requirements to select a robust machine, with ease of portability for demonstration, with all the previously given wish list of requirements, my processor/reactor chose itself – As will yours when you factor in your own specific requirements.

My research led me to Groningen in the Netherlands, or as I know it, Holland.

There I discovered a company with a passion for its product, and with its ongoing research & development, daily striving to be the best in the industry.

So for me the machine that comes the closest to my personal wish list has to be the Biodys Engineering's model C300 processor/reactor, thermostatically controlled version with its CE rated equipment & many built in safety factors, high quality construction taking into account the ATEX directives with the best dollar for dollar real value, that I have found anywhere.

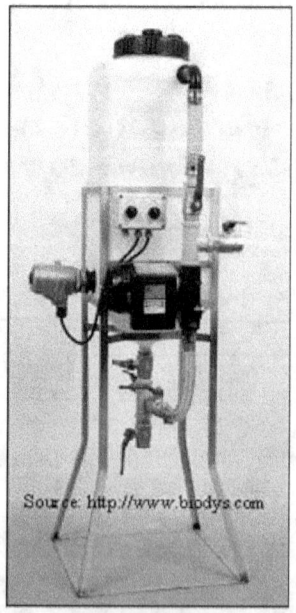

Source: http://www.biodys.com

Figure 19

In my opinion engineering wise the C300-R50 processor is a winner, safe, compact, light, strong and efficient, with a built in wash/dry system.

1x50 Litre HDPE tank in steel frame and stand.

1 clever & separate 14 litre HDPE, methoxide mixing tank, with manual stir and injector.

1x1.2KW low density heating element with thermostat CE certified

1x370W 40I/min fuel pump CE certified

1xElectric control panel IP56

1xSpray wash head

The C300-R50 Numbers

40 Litres biodiesel = 8.8 Imperial gallons per run daily = 8.8 x 5 = 44 Imp gallons for 5 day week.

40 Litres biodiesel = 10.6 US gallons per run daily = 10.6 x 5 = 53 US gallons for 5 day week.

Therefore, on these figures you can produce 10,000 litres per annum with Biodys C300-R50 processor, if you prefer 2,200 Imperial gallons per ann. – that is 2,642 US gallons per annum.

Of if you like 200 litres (44 UK gallons) or (53 US gallons) weekly without any additional equipment.

This company, Biodys Engineering, have a terrific range of processors, and complete solutions to all your manufacturing questions and/or needs which you can check at
http://www.biodys.com

I use this company as a good example because of my experience in owning and using their equipment, and observing the in house expertise and advice given, as to what to expect from the professionals in this field.

In due course I will be reviewing other manufactures equipment and services in the future, along with the Appleseed parts, vegetable oils new or reclaimed as well as chemical suppliers and a host of incidentals. (See page 237)

Biodiesel in larger quantities

If you do need larger quantities of biodiesel daily then you can simply add extra settling tanks so as to process more runs quickly, or add a Biodys Engineering's own dry wash filter system using their own superb filtering and cleaning agent, made with their own secret recipe, using natural magnesium aluminium silicate enriched with bleaching earth powder.

Biodys product is called Magnidon™ and using it about doubles the output of your processor with its fast dry/wash cycle efficiency, it avoids the use of the water wash cycle and making it possible to purify crude biodiesel into EN14214 quality fast.

With no need for wash water it's another plus to our environment as it helps with the ever present risk of water shortages.

So as you can see whatever model you choose by adding extra settling tanks and/or the Magnidon dry wash system, every processor can greatly increase its actual biodiesel output efficiency.

Obviously you normally buy bigger processors to produce larger quantities of biodiesel because there would be less work involved plus normally it is a more economic way.

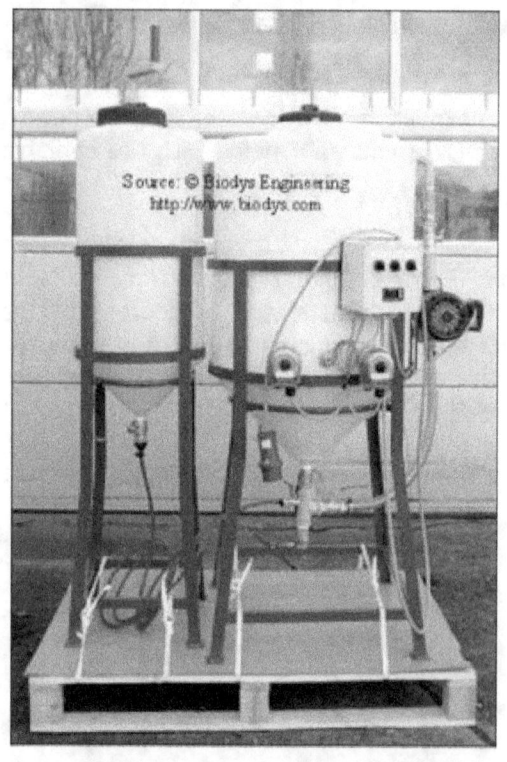

Source: © Biodys Engineering
http://www.biodys.com

Biodys Engineering has a terrific range to cope with all requirements and I suspect the next

size up, the C1200-R200 is capable of some 57,000 litres per annum (12,538 Imperial UK gallons per annum or 15,057 US gallons per annum) and may be the most popular reactor among the public and small businesses.

However whatever your equipment, you can expand output according to changing requirements very easily.

This photograph is of my own my Biodys C300-R50 processor/reactor which can produce 44 Imp gallons of biodiesel in a 5 day week without breaking sweat and a lot more if you really need to do so, simply by following the information and techniques taught within these pages.

So in conclusion as to which processor/reactor or which machine manufacturer you choose, taking into account your personal requirements, financial restraints or otherwise, just remember to think ahead, do your own research on your potential requirement and look around for realistic opportunities.

Think laterally, that is to say if you really only want to make enough for your own needs and yet find the ideal machine is at this moment a little too costly, then perhaps two or three friends could club together to purchase your ideal and have an agreed rota as to use; say alternate days or third day for own use or whatever ... Get the idea?

What I am saying is . . . with a little thought a positive way forward can be worked out allowing anyone to get to use good equipment etc!

Custom Design

Any Manufacturer worth its salt is able to get its design team behind your needs and requirements, and this shows long term commitment.

Even larger output processors like the Biodys C6000 / R1000 for example has 1000 litres processing tank, which has a 5 times larger capacity than the C1200.

However if you are really looking for major production, check out Biodys.com website where you will see the M2, the first MX plant.

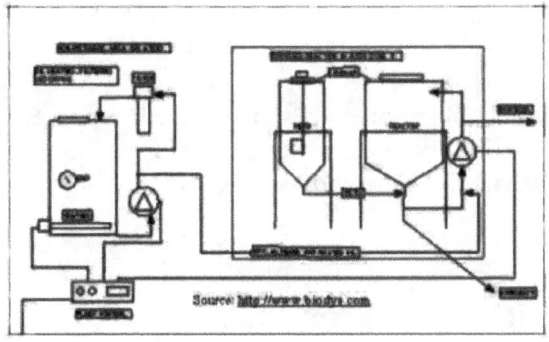

Figure 20
Deliberately out of focus

No matter where you buy your equipment or your choice of manufacturer, just remember the basic rules when checking them all out, and remember above all enjoy yourselves; a little care at this stage will stand you in good stead for many a year.

Chapter 12
How to get involved

Want to know how you can stay on top of the latest information, and take part in biodiesel's future? That's what this chapter is all about!

After the success of the 2005 National Biodiesel Conference & Expo in Fort Lauderdale, Florida, and others in 06, 07, & 08, the next the National Biodiesel Conference & Expo 2009 will be in San Francisco, California and annually into the future. *http://www.biodieselconference*.org

Additional Resources

Beyond this book, here are some great sources of information:

The National Biodiesel Board: *www.biodiesel.org*

US Department of Energy:
www.eere.energy.gov/afdc/index.html

Northwest Biodiesel Network:*www.nwbiodiesel.org*

National Renewable Energy Laboratory:
www.nrel.gov

US Department of Energy: *http://www.energy.gov*

Material Safety Data Sheets:
- *www.jtbaker.com*
- *www.mallbaker.com*
- *http://hazard.com/msds/*

Fuel Specs:
- *www.biofuelsystems.com/specification.htm*
- *http://ec.europa.eu/geninfo/query/resultaction.jsp?userinput=biodieselhttp://www.biodiesel.org/resources/fuelfactsheets/standards_and_warranties.shtm*
- *www.bebioenergy.com/http://www.deh.gov.au/atmosphere/fuelquality/standards/biodiesel/index.html*

The Tax Man USA: *www.irs.gov*

Tax Enquiries UK: *www.hmrc.gov.uk/*

ATEX Directives:
http://en.wikipedia.org/wiki/ATEX_directive

Magnidon™ Filter Agent Suppliers:
www.biodys.com

BioDiesel Filling Stations:
www.biodieselfillingstations.co.uk

BioDiesel Filling Stations:
www.biodieselfillingstations.co.uk

Use search engines to find suppliers for your location, such as Apple-seed parts & reclaimed vegetable oil specialist: *www.oilco.co.uk*

Articles

I publish articles on many subjects by RSS feeds, as well as whatever else I find interesting at the time on **my blog *www.mervrees.com***

I hope they will be of interest to you.

I will advise you either via my blog or website ***www.whybiodiesel.com*** or if you wish you can get free newsletters, or emails by opting in at ***www.mervtech.com*** obviously for you to accept or reject at will.

Why not check out my very own private research tool by watching my Free Video Tutorial at ***www.geniesearcher.com***

Books

Several new books in either Soft Back and/or eBook form on varying subjects are in the pipeline, so if I may, as and when I publish any new work, I will advise you again via my website or by my free newsletter /email if you have opted-in at www.MervTech.com obviously for you to accept or reject at will at any time.

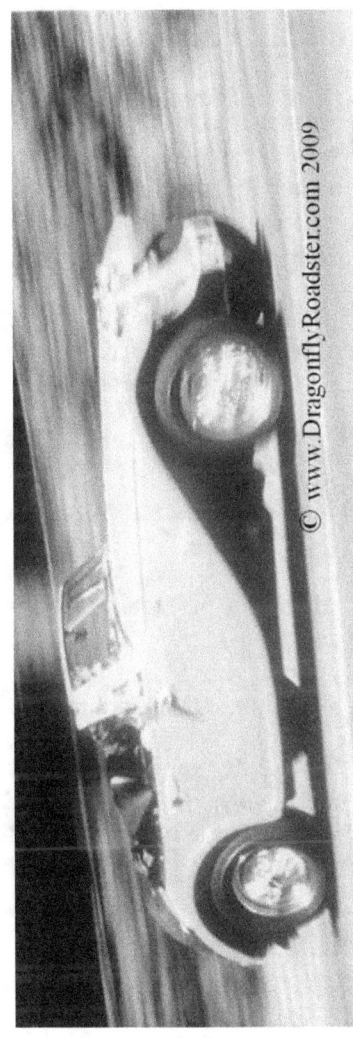

Figure 21

Jacquie putting her Dragonfly Roadster through its paces in publicity shoot for my original Dragonfly
sales brochure in 1984.

Now her family's restaurant in 2009 helps the biodieselers with the waste cooking oils for their biodiesel requirements.

© www.Dragonfly-Roadster.com 2009

Conclusion

In 1912 Dr. Rudolf Diesel said: "The use of vegetable oils for engine fuels may seem insignificant today. But such oils may become in the course of time as important as the petroleum and coal tar products of the present time".

Dr. Diesel was right, because biodiesel is more than just an alternative fuel; it is a vision of the past that has brought forth an inspired present and a hopeful future.

Therefore, without question, it will be interesting to watch how biodiesel grows and flourishes in society.

Having reached the end of the first part of your biodiesel journey with your own copy of "The Book on Biodiesel" firmly in your grasp, you can go forward and start with a whole new look at life.

You now have a better understanding of this renewable environment friendly diesel fuel, the knowledge to manufacture it for yourself, and knowing its importance in preserving the quality of living in the present and future environment, for the people of the world.

With these tools and understanding that you have gained from your new manual, you have every opportunity to embrace the present and the growing future of biodiesel, and even get involved in the industry, saving you and your family's budget, and go on to a more profitable future.

You are now ready to start thinking outside the smog of the present; it is time to start looking at vegetable oil in a whole new light as the sun filters through you can now put your newly acquired knowledge into action!

Just remember to have fun, as you go forward gently 'Step by Step' with every success in your new venture.

Happy motoring!

Merv Rees.

International Biodiesel Day

August 10th

Honouring Dr. Rudolf Diesel

'The Founder of Biodiesel'

Appendix I

The Biodiesel Glossary

Alcohol – a large classification of organic compounds containing one or more hydroxyl groups attached to carbon atoms.

Algae – chiefly aquatic, eukaryotic one-celled or multi-cellular plants without true systems, roots and leaves that are typically autotrophic, photosynthetic, and contain chlorophyll. Algae are not typically found in groundwater. Source: www.nsc.org/ehc/glossary.htm

Alkali – a classification of substances that liberate hydroxide ions in water, to form caustic and corrosive solutions which turn litmus paper blue, with a pH higher than 7, for example sodium Hydroxide, a compound that reacts with or neutralizes hydrogen ions.

Alternative Fuel – Methanol, denatured ethanol, and other alcohols; mixtures containing 85% or more by volume of methanol, denatured ethanol, and other alcohols with gasoline or other fuels; natural gas; liquefied petroleum gas; hydrogen; coal-derived liquid fuels; non-alcohol fuels (such as biodiesel) derived from biological material; and electricity. 'P-Series' fuels were added to this list since the original definition in EPAct.

Anhydrous – "Without water" – transesterification of biodiesel must be an anhydrous process or funny things happen. Water in the vegetable oil causes either no reaction or cloudy biodiesel, and water in lye or methanol renders it less useful or even useless, depending on how much water is present. Either let your vegetable oil settle for 2-3 days before using and drain the water off the bottom, or heat the oil and boil off the water. Make sure to store lye and methanol in separate airtight containers.

ATEX – There are two ATEX Directives that concern us
  • ATEX equipment directive 94/9/EC – see Additional Resources
  • ATEX workplace directive 99/92/EC – see Additional Resources

B100 – 100% pure biodiesel.

B20 – A blend of biodiesel fuel with petroleum-based diesel where 20% of the volume is biodiesel. B5, B10, B50 etc simply refers to the percentage by volume of biodiesel added to regular diesel.

Biodiesel – "Biofuel" "McDiesel" – An environmentally safe, low-putting fuel for most diesel internal combustion and turbine engines. Can be mixed with petroleum fuel and stored anywhere petroleum is. Made from fresh or waste vegetable oils (triglycerides) that are a renewable energy source. Both commercially and privately made around the world. Relatively safe and easy to process when conscientiously approached. Benefits are substantially reduced engine emissions with as little as 20% biodiesel with 80% petroleum.

Biodiesel Plants – Refers to the larger biodiesel reactor sites.

Burning – the rapid oxidization of a substance in a manner that releases thermal energy

Burette / Buret – A calibrated glass tube used clamped upright, with a tap at the bottom. Used to deliver small measured amounts of liquid, e.g. during titration.

Canola – Cultivars of oilseed rape – rape seed

Carbon – a common non-metallic element, occurring naturally as diamond, charcoal and graphite. Carbon is one of the most important elements for the development of life, and the storage of energy.

Carbon cycle – the continuous process of combining and releasing carbon and oxygen thereby storing and emitting heat and energy. Catabolism + anabolism = metabolism.

Cold Flow – The tendency of a pressure sensitive adhesive to act as a heavy viscous liquid over long periods of time. Such phenomena as oozing and increase in adhesion with time are the result of this characteristic.

Combustion – a reaction in which a substance produces heat or light by combination with oxygen, producing an oxide.

De-Ionized Water – is water that lacks ions, such as cations from sodium, calcium, iron, copper and anions such as chloride and bromide. This means it has been purified from all other ions but H+ or more correctly H3O+ and OH-, but it may still contain other non-ionic types of impurities such as organic compounds (www.wikipedia.org)

Diesel (petrodiesel) – non-volatile mineral fuel with a high flash point used in compression ignition engines, as invented by Dr. Rudolf Diesel in 1895, originally running on peanut oil. The name of the inventor was then transferred by the petrochemical industry to the fossil fuel that became the substitute for the organic oils for which this form of engine was originally developed.

Distilled Water – is water that has had virtually all of its impurities removed through distillation (boiling the water and re-condensing the steam into liquid water). (www.wikipedia.org)

Esters – a product of the reaction of acids (usually organic) and alcohols. CH_3COOCH_3 – methyl acetate is the simplest ester. One of the oxygen's has a double bond you can replace the 'CH3' part on the right with more CH_2 chunks, and you get other methyl esters, including biodiesel's methyl stearate. Many of the esters smell good.

Ethanol – C_2H_6O an organic alcohol also called ethyl alcohol, formed when fermenting sugars or glycerine.

FAME – Fatty Acid Methyl Ester – (FAME) created by an alkali catalyzed reaction between fats or fatty acids and methanol.

Fat – A classification of natural esters of glycerol, and fatty acids existing as solids at room temperature.

Feedstock (for biodiesel) – Oil-seed crops which produce the oils used in biodiesel production, e.g. sunflower oil, corn oil, cottonseed oil, canola oil, mustard oil, soybean oil, a variety of edible rapeseed oil, palm oil, etc

FFA – Free Fatty Acids or FF are acids that form from heat, oxidation or water from the foods that have been cooked in the oil.

Fossil – Remains of organic materials, subsequently buried within the earth's crust, often carbonized as a result of intense heat and / or pressure.

Fossil Fuels – Crude oil from wells around the world.
For example, regular diesel is a petro-diesel.

Free – Liberated – In the case of triglycerides, meaning the fatty acid hydrocarbon chains are detached from glycerol, and thereby become free fatty acids.

Glycerine/Glycerol – C3H8O3, a sweet greasy organic substance, produced as a result of hydrolyzing triglycerides.

Grease – Oily or fatty matter, normally of organic origin, consisting of hydrocarbon chains.

HDPE – High Density Polyethylene. Used in heavy duty plastic containers etc.

Hydrocarbon – A compound of hydrogen and carbon often occurs as long atomic chains in which each carbon atom is attached to two hydrogen atoms forming a long chain. They store a great deal of energy.

Hydrogen - H – The lightest gaseous element, and simplest of all atoms, occurring rarely in nature as a single atom, but common in the form of water, and in all organic compounds

Isopropyl Alcohol – Or Isopropanol is a common name for propan-2-ol, a colourless, flammable chemical compound with a strong odour. (www.wikipedia.org)

Life-cycle analysis – A total valuation of a process in which all the inputs and outcomes of a reaction are fully considered.

Lipid – A classification of organic compounds, including fatty acids, oils, waxes and steroids that are insoluble in water, but soluble in organic solvents.

Litmus – A dye extracted from lichen, used as a pH indicator. The indicator is supplied as a paper treated with the dye. It is available in two types: blue litmus paper turns red under acidic conditions, whereas red litmus paper turns blue under alkaline conditions. In either case the colour change occurs over the 4.5 – 8.3 pH range.

Lubricity – Refers to the lubricant value associated with a fuel. In the case of biodiesel, it is much higher than fossil-based petro-diesels, thereby giving greater engine life and quieter, cooler running.

Lye – NaOH, sodium hydroxide (see sodium hydroxide)

KOH - Potassium hydroxide (see potassium hydroxide)

Lye-Water – 0.1% NaOH (sodium hydroxide / lye) solution in water (i.e. 1 in 1000 dilution). Also applies to a solution of KOH (potassium hydroxide / lye) in same proportions.

Magnesol® – (Registered trademark of the Dallas Group of America Inc)
Synthetic magnesium silicate absorbent an absorbent filter aid.

Magnidon™ – natural magnesium aluminium silicate enriched bleaching earth powder a filter aid specially developed for waterless biodiesel cleaning.

Methanol – Also known as methyl alcohol or wood alcohol, chemical formula CH3OH methanol is a highly volatile, flammable colourless liquid, and is toxic.

Methoxide (biodiesel expression) – Is the mixing together, in the correct proportions, of methanol and lye as part of the procedure in the manufacture of biodiesel. This mixture is in fact a methyl ester.

My research always led me to believe that biodieselers hat it all taped down when it came to the so called simple chemistry of manufacturing biodiesel from waste vegetable oil or straight vegetable oils!

Like many things in life, the first main manufacturers who advertise their name or brand heavily, the name becomes the product, then generally late comers to the party, have all their similar products called by the original brand name.

A good example is vacuum cleaners – yes that's right we call them all 'Hoovers'!

See what I mean?

That is exactly how it happens when a given name or process is wrongly named in the first instance. As is the case with biodieselers who in the main learnt their new skills by word of mouth, or reading books, or as often now via the internet, and quite naturally use terms that they have been given or have read in their research.

*{According to 'Wikipedia', referring to the product of mixing methanol and sodium hydroxide as "methoxide" is incorrect. Nevertheless, throughout the biodiesel production community, this is the name that is used. In actual fact a methoxide is a

type of chemical, and we are referring to a specific chemical by the group name. This is much the same as when we refer to "salt" when we are in fact talking about sodium chloride.}*

Mono-Alkyl Esters (fatty acids) – These are derived from animal fats or vegetable oils.

NO_x – A form of nitrous oxide – Powerful greenhouse gas emissions given out by combustion engines, not to be confused with N_2O – Laughing gas.

Oleochemical – chemical compounds derived from biological oils or fats.

Oil – a broad range of inflammable and often, volatile organic compounds insoluble in water but soluble in organic solvents. In biological systems, fat that is liquid at room temperature (20°C)

Oral Syringe – A non needle type of syringe for use in measuring liquids, and are available in chemists/drug stores.

Oxidation – burning in oxygen, normally highly exothermic (heat releasing), but also any increase in oxidization sate, (i.e. loss of electrons). This results in the formation of an oxide, rusting or corroding.

Peak Oil – Refers to the time when we reach the maximum worldwide extraction of fossil fuels, and from then on the clock is ticking for world stocks declining.

Petrochemical – Substances derived from the winning of fossil hydrocarbons, in the form of crude oil or natural gas, and tars.

pH – A measure of the acidity or alkalinity of a substance. Neutral pH is 7 (neither acidic nor alkaline), lower pH indicates acidity and high numbers indicate alkalinity.

Phenolphthalein – pH indicator used in acid-base titrations, it turns pink when in presence of an alkali.

Phenol Red – pH indicator used in acid-base titrations. Turns pink/red for around 30 seconds or so, then returns to a yellow colour.

Photosynthesis – The process used within living organisms by which energy from the sun is stored in carbohydrates made from carbon dioxide and water, using chlorophyll from plants. It is the major natural energy collecting reaction, occurring mainly in plants. Plants use chlorophyll to capture solar energy within the chemical bonds of synthesized sugar molecules. The process effectively reduced carbon dioxide and water to produce sugar and oxygen. Plants then synthesize other sugars, proteins, DNA, starch, cellulose and fats from these simple hexose sugars.

Pipette – Eye-dropper sometimes used for making small test samples of biodiesel.

Potassium Hydroxide – Also known as Lye or potash-lye, chemical formula KOH.

Processor – See Reactor

Rape – Rape seed – rape seed oil – Food grade oil produced from rapeseed is called Canola oil. Canola is the name taken from "Canada oil" due to the fact that much of the development of the oil was performed in Canada. Another early term for this oil is Colza.

Reactor – Main equipment for manufacturing biodiesel, also known as a processor.

REE – Rapeseed ethyl esters.

RME – Rapeseed methyl ester. The form of fuel created by transesterifying fat as a Fatty Acid Methyl Ester, or FAME

Sodium Hydroxide – Also known as lye or caustic soda, chemical formula NaOH. It is a caustic metallic base generally a white crystalline powder, which reacts violently in water.

Soy – Soy Oil, a vegetable oil pressed from soybeans.

SVO – Straight vegetable oil. – Unused vegetable oil, which can be the main ingredient of our fuel.

Tax Incentives – In general, a means of employing the tax code to stimulate investment in or development of a socially desirable economic objective without direct expenditure from the budget of a given unit of government. Such incentives can take the form of tax exemptions or credits.

Titration – Applied to biodiesel, titration is the act of determining the acidity of a sample of WVO by the drop-wise addition of a known base to the sample while testing with pH paper for the desired neutral pH=7 reading. The amount of base needed to neutralize an amount of WVO determines how much base to add to the entire batch.

Transesterification – The process of making bio-diesel by the separation of the three hydrocarbon chains from a lipid triglyceride to form glycerol, and bio-diesel, or the catalyst splitting the oil into two parts.

Viscosity – How a liquid is resistant to flow; "thickness" or "thinness". methanol has a low viscosity, while vegetable oil has a high viscosity.

Washing (biodiesel expression) – Four types:

1. Mist washing sometimes called spray washing down through biodiesel.

2. Bubble washing – air bubbles rising in water up & through your biodiesel.

3. Stir Washing – Adding water and thoroughly stirring.

4. Dry washing – filtering biodiesel through synthetic or natural magnesium silicate absorbent

WVO – Waste vegetable oil. The used oil we collect from fry's shops and restaurants etc, which can be a main ingredient of our fuel.

Some Sources of definitions:

www.bio-power.co.uk/glossary.htm

http://biodiesel.infopop.cc/groupee/forums/a/tpc/f/829605551/m/270600361

www.google.ca/search?hl=en&lr=&oi=defmore&q=define:cold+flow

www.eere.energy.gov/afdc

www.wikipedia.org

Appendix II
Sources Cited

Figure 1, page 21
www.whybiodiesel.com Version of (Source:
http://biodiesel.org/resources/faqs/default.shtm/)

Figure 2, page 40
http://energyquest.ca.gov/scientists/diesel.html

Figure 3, page 57
*www.eere.energy.gov/afdc/pdfs/biodiesel_chart.pd
f/*

Figure 4, page 58
*www.biodiesel.org/pdf_files/fuelfactsheets/Producti
on.PDF*

Figure 5, page 59
www.whybiodiesel.com

Figure 6, page 71
www.whybiodiesel.com

Figure 7, page 79
www.whybiodiesel.com

Figure 8, page 85
www.whybiodiesel.com

Figure 9, page 87
www.whybiodiesel.com

Figure 10, page 108
www.whybiodiesel.com

Figure 11, page 150
*www.afdc.energy.gov/afdc/vehicles/emissions_bio
diesel.html*

Figure 12, page 152
www.biodiesel.org &
www.whybiodiesel.com

Figure 13, page 154
*www.eere.energy.gov/vehiclesandfuels/pdfs/basics
/jtb_biodiesel.pdf*

Figure 14, page 172
www.eia.doe.gov/

Figure 15, page 188
*www.biodiesel.org/pdf_files/fuelfactsheets/BDSpec
.PDF*

Figure 16, page 199
www.nrel.gov/docs/legosti/fy98/24190.pdf

Figure 17, page 202
www.nrel.gov/docs/legosti/fy98/24190.pdf

Figure 18, page 206
www.hubbertpeak.com/de/lecture/html

Figure 19, page 230

www.biodys.com

Figure 20, page 237
www.biodys.com

Figure 21, page 241
www.mervtech.com/oursites/dragonfly

Links for:

Material Safety Data Sheets Source, pages 51-52
www.mallbaker.com

Yellowstone Park, page 214
- *http://deq.mt.gov/Energy/bioenergy/*
- *www.deq.state.mt.us/Energy/bioenergy/Tr uckInTheParkBiodieselDemo.asp*
- *http://deq.mt.gov/Energy/bioenergy/imag es/trkSide3.jpg*

I would like to take this opportunity to thank all groups, companies and/or individuals who have so generously allowed me to use their source materials in helping to clarify this important subject and its potential significance to our environment.

About the Author

For Mervyn Rees, it all began with a seven year engineering apprenticeship starting in 1949, which at that time, meant working in every department of the industry. Following that came three interesting years in the Royal Air Force at the request of Her Majesty the Queen.

In 1959, came the business side of Mervyns' career, take your pick, each of his companies he built from scratch over the years. Starting in Garages, Workshops & Petrol Forecourts, and growing over the years to; Tyre Importers, Wholesalers & Retailers, Trailer Manufacturer & Importers, Exhibition Units Designer, Commercial & Private Property Developer, Promotion Company Registered Motor Vehicle Manufacturer (Dragonfly Roadsters), and a Nursing Home which he finally sold and opened his own Health Clinic.

After a major spinal injury in 1976, Mervyn's interest focused on the health profession and so he retrained becoming a health professional with evolving characteristics. He started in Psychology, gaining diplomas in Psychotherapy &

Hypnotherapy, then needing other skills to help himself rehabilitate, he would train as required, qualifying with diplomas as; Fitness Trainer & Sports Injury & Rehabilitation Therapist, Nutritionist, then The International Institute of Health & Holistic Therapies, Kinesiology and Advanced Bowen Technique Practitioner and is recognized as a highly skilled rehabilitation specialist.

At this point, being certain in his ability to help himself and others around him, he was invited to become an NHS (National Health Service) Independent Provider, as well as a BUPA registered therapist.

In 1988, Mervyn had the honour of being elected a Fellow and became a Fellow of the Institute of the Motor Industry.

Towards retirement, he volunteered to go to, war torn Bosnia Herzegovina, where he used his medical skills in rehabilitation, helping anyone who needed him at his own expense and absolutely free to everyone, off and on over a period of several years. His work in rehabilitation involves him in treating all sections of society, in whatever part of the world he may be, in all sorts of situations; refugee camps, hospitals, clinics, individual homes, or in the 'great outdoors', in fact, anywhere at all.

The idea was to run his health clinic until retirement, but having retired, people still come to his door from time to time, with requests for help, which he always willingly gives. Retirement for some can be daunting after such a busy life, but to others like Mervyn, it is an exciting new crossroad.

Having celebrated his 74th birthday, as usual, his way to relax was to find something new to interest him, and finding the magic of the internet, he could communicate to a far wider horizon. After more than fifty years in industry, and a lifetime of extensive experience, Mervyn is still very busy.

Now taking a sabbatical for a couple years, he indulges his great interest in wildlife and the countryside, his love of boating, angling, painting in watercolours, and writing as well as making whatever in his workshop.

He will gladly give talks on his experiences, as well as talk about various therapies and disciplines he works in, environmentally friendly fuels, your health and the motor industry. In fact, he just loves to talk about whatever is of interest to you.

Notes